Oliver Goldsmith Revisited

Twayne's English Authors Series

Arthur F. Kinney, Editor

University of Massachusetts, Amherst

TEAS 487

OLIVER GOLDSMITH
Portrait by Sir Joshua Reynolds. Courtesy of Lord Sackville.

Oliver Goldsmith Revisited

Peter Dixon

Queen Mary and Westfield College, University of London

Twayne Publishers • Boston
A Division of G. K. Hall & Co.

Publisher's Note

Oliver Goldsmith Revisited by Peter Dixon is a timely retrospective of Goldsmith's life and works, taking into account the scholarship that has surrounded Goldsmith since 1967, when Twayne Publishers issued *Oliver Goldsmith* by Clara M. Kirk. We are pleased to offer this new evaluation of Goldsmith's achievement.

Published by Twayne Publishers
A division of G. K. Hall & Co.
70 Lincoln Street
Boston, Massachusetts 02111

Copyediting supervised by Barbara Sutton.
Book production by Janet Z. Reynolds.
Book design by Barbara Anderson.
Typeset by Graphic Sciences Corp., Cedar Rapids, Iowa.

10 9 8 7 6 5 4 3 2 1

Library of Congress Cataloging-in-Publication Data

Dixon, Peter, 1932-
    Oliver Goldsmith revisited / Peter Dixon.
      p.   cm. — (Twayne's English authors series ; TEAS 487)
    Includes bibliographical references (p.   ) and index.
    ISBN 0-8057-7008-9
    1. Goldsmith, Oliver, 1728-1774—Criticism and interpretation.
I. Title. II. Series.
PR3494.D58   1991
828'.609—dc20   91-7819

Contents

Preface

Oliver Goldsmith has always been a source of puzzlement. His contemporaries, despairing of finding rational consistency in someone who seemed to make a point of not behaving as a man of letters should, amply registered their bewilderment. Boswell, who first met Goldsmith on Christmas Day 1762, set him down as "odd" and "curious." Johnson found an inexplicable gap between the inept conversationalist and the elegant, moral writer: "No man was more foolish when he had not a pen in his hand, or more wise when he had." Many people suspected that he was not the author of the works published under his name. Others, like Mrs. Thrale, patronized him as the "poor dear Doctor." "Lord bless us," she soliloquized in her diary, "what an anomalous Character was his. . . . A man made up of Contradictions—Knowledge & Ignorance, Artlessness and Design, Delicacy & Grossness." "Artlessness and Design": Mrs. Thrale neatly identifies one of the central problems—how to do justice to Goldsmith's humor. In his conversation as in his writing he exploited a sly, teasing kind of humor that eluded the grasp of his hearers, as it continues to elude the awkward fingers of criticism.

> This dog and man at first were friends,
> But when a pique began,
> The dog, to gain some private ends,
> Went mad and bit the man.

The original version of this stanza (in the first edition of *The Vicar of Wakefield*) reads "to gain his private ends." The substitution of "some" for "his" is a stroke of comic genius; the poet hints darkly and vaguely at those inscrutable "ends" as though, by contrast, the dog's going mad were some mundanely ordinary and explicable event. But to attempt to analyze such a delightfully delicate joke is to coarsen and flatten it.

His work inevitably continues to perplex. Is he a sentimentalist or an opponent of sentiment? Is he a hard-hitting satirist in the tradition of Swift and Pope, or an amiable humorist, or a writer so various that he cannot be pinned down and labeled as a specimen of one kind or the other? How deep and significant are his Irish roots? His Irishness has been neglected, since all his published work appeared after he had left his native country, and is only now being explored by such critics as Seamus Deane, W. J. McCormack, and (in a forthcoming biography) Samuel H. Woods. And we remain uncertain as to what Goldsmith actually wrote. New candidates for the canon spring up almost annually, while some doubtful pieces (my own prime suspects are "The History of Miss Stanton" and "On the Different Schools of Music") continue to be accepted as genuine.

Clara Kirk, the author of the first Twayne's English Authors Series volume on Goldsmith, was clearly fascinated by her subject's double nature: rational, witty, ironically critical, yet also solitary and melancholy. Her investigations, however, were hampered by their having to rely on J. W. M. Gibbs's late-nineteenth-century edition of Goldsmith's works. The immense, and immensely erudite editorial labors of Arthur Friedman bore fruit, in the five-volume *Collected Works* of 1966, just too late for her to use. All subsequent students of Goldsmith are heavily indebted to Friedman for his clarification of bibliographical obscurities, his scrupulous work on the canon, and his establishment of a sound text. It may therefore seem like "graceless obstinacy," in Goldsmith's phrase, that I have decided not to quote from his edition. Friedman's editorial policy is tightly conservative in matters of punctuation, spelling, and typography, and his choice of readings, in texts that Goldsmith revised, does not always command assent. Though I have studied Goldsmith in his monumental edition and have been gratefully guided by it through the bibliographical tangles, I have decided to offer here a modernized and, on rare occasions, emended text, based on the early editions. For convenience of reference, however, I have keyed my quotations wherever possible to the *Collected Works*. In citing Goldsmith's letters, his sister's biographical narrative, and the invaluable "Portrait" by Sir Joshua Reynolds, I have accepted the emendations and additions (without the square brackets) of the editors of these texts, and have silently expanded abbreviations and added a little punctuation.

I am grateful to Lord Sackville for permission to reproduce the Reynolds portrait of Goldsmith at Knole; to the Courtauld Institute for making available the photograph of the portrait; and to the Huntington Library for photocopies of its file of the *Weekly Magazine*. My thanks, for their help and advice, to Pauline Caslin (of the Irish Tourist Board, Dublin), Vicky Bancroft, David Bindman, and all the enthusiasts for Goldsmith with whom I have discussed the man and his writings over the years. I owe a special debt to Rosemary Clarke-Jones, Blanche Litwin, Jenny Allen, Bob Grainger, Jay Hammond, Brian Place, and Dawn Pudney for getting a difficult manuscript into a publishable form, and to Professor Bertram H. Davis for scrutinizing it with most helpful care.

Chronology

1731?   Oliver Goldsmith born 10 November at Pallas (County Longford) or Smith Hill (County Roscommon), Ireland, fifth child of Ann and Rev. Charles Goldsmith. Family moves to Lissoy.

1737–1745   Attends schools at Lissoy, Elphin, Athlone, and Edgeworthstown.

1745   Admitted to Trinity College, Dublin, on 11 June.

1747   Father dies.

1750   Graduates (B.A.) in February. Works as tutor. Abortive plans to enter church or legal profession.

1752   Enters Edinburgh University as medical student.

1754   Travels to Holland to continue medical studies at Leiden.

1755   Travels on foot to Paris, then to Germany, Switzerland, and northern Italy, whence he returns through France.

1756   Arrives in England, early February. Works as an apothecary's assistant in London. Briefly sets up as a medical practitioner. Employed as teacher in Peckham.

1757   Begins literary career by writing reviews for *Monthly Review,* April to September.

1758   *The Memoirs of a Protestant* (translation) published 9 March. Appointed civilian physician to East India Company. Begins "Memoirs of Voltaire," published in *Lady's Magazine,* February–November 1761.

1759   Writes reviews for Smollett's *Critical Review,* January–March 1760. *An Inquiry into the Present State of Polite Learning in Europe* published 4 April. The *Bee* (periodical), issued weekly from 6 October to 24 November. Contributes to various magazines. Meets Thomas Percy and Samuel Johnson.

1760   The "Chinese Letters" appear in Newbery's *Public Ledger,* 24 January–14 August 1761. Continues to write miscellaneous journalism.

1761   Meets Sir Joshua Reynolds.

1762   Writes essays for *Lloyd's Evening Post. The Citizen of the World* published 1 May. Sells manuscript of *The Vicar of Wakefield* for publication. Visits Bath and Tunbridge. *The Life of Richard Nash* published 14 October. Meets James Boswell.

1764   Becomes original member of The Club, formed by Reynolds and Johnson. *An History of England in a Series of Letters* published 26 June. "The Traveller, or A Prospect of Society" published 19 December.

1765   *Essays by Mr. Goldsmith* published 14 June. *Edwin and Angelina* privately printed for the countess of Northumberland. Briefly resumes medical practice.

1766   *The Vicar of Wakefield* published 27 March. *Essays,* second edition, revised and augmented. *Poems for Young Ladies* (anthology) published 15 December.

1767   *The Beauties of English Poesy* (anthology) published 6 April.

1768   *The Good-Natured Man* performed at Covent Garden 29 January, and published 5 February. Moves, after a variety of residences in and about London, to 2, Brick Court, The Temple. Elder brother, Henry, dies in May.

1769   Contracts to write a "new Natural History of Animals, etc. . . . in eight volumes." *The Roman History* published 18 May. Nominated professor of ancient history in the newly founded Royal Academy.

1770   "The Deserted Village" published 26 May. "The Life of Parnell," prefixed to Parnell's *Poems on Several Occasions,* published in June. Visits Paris during summer with Horneck family. Mother dies. Growing friendship with Viscount Clare and family; writes "The Haunch of Venison" (published 1776). *Life of Bolingbroke* published 1 December.

1771   *The History of England . . . to the Death of George II* published 6 August.

1772   *Threnodia Augustalis* performed and published 20 February. Suffers serious illness during August, caused by bladder infection.

1773   Contributes essays to *Westminster Magazine,* January and March, including "An Essay on the Theatre." *She Stoops to Conquer* performed at Covent Garden 15 March and published 25 March. *The Grumbler* (one-act farce) performed at Covent Garden 8 May. Projects a "Universal Dictionary of Arts and Sciences." In ill health during summer.

1774   Writes "Retaliation" (published 19 April). Suffers from fever and kidney disease during March. Dies 4 April, at Brick Court. Buried in Temple churchyard 9 April. *The Grecian History* published 15 June. *An History of the Earth and Animated Nature* published 30 June.

1776   Commemorated by Nollekens's monument, with Johnson's epitaph, in Westminster Abbey.

Chapter One

Early Years: The Search for Recognition

In September 1752 the British government brought itself into line with Continental methods of timekeeping, and belatedly accepted the Gregorian calendar. The population had to adjust to the loss of 11 days from 1752, and to the fact that future years would begin on 1 January instead of 25 March. Those who lived through this temporal discontinuity may be excused for being uncertain as to when exactly they were born. Goldsmith was in this condition. In the spring of 1773 Thomas Percy, a friend of some 14 years' standing, sought biographical information from the subject's own mouth; Goldsmith told him that he had been born on 29 November 1731, or perhaps it was 1730. His elder sister Catherine, who later wrote an account of his early years, offered 10 November 1729, and confirmation of that day of the month came when Sir James Prior, Goldsmith's first systematic biographer, inspected the family Bible, whose flyleaves recorded important domestic events; unfortunately the year in question was indecipherable. Some vague and inconsistent references in Goldsmith's letters, together with alternative suggestions by other members of the family, mean that every year from 1727 to 1731 has had its advocates. We may reasonably settle for the one that first sprang to Goldsmith's lips when he talked to Percy: 1731.[1]

The place of birth too is uncertain. The Bible flyleaf nominates Pallas, a hamlet near the shore of Lough Ree, in the very center of Ireland. A tradition carefully nurtured by his mother's side of the family asserted that he was born at his grandmother's house at Smith Hill (now Ardnagowan), near what was then the large village of Elphin. What is certain is that the family into which Goldsmith was born, together with its friends and connections, formed a small but well-established and closely knit clerical community. Catherine refers to "all the friends of his family who were all in the Church."[2] His father, Charles, a curate when Oliver was born, was shortly afterward appointed rector at Lissoy, a village eight miles from Pallas. The boy's uncle, Thomas Contarine, was a clergyman at Kilmore. More distantly, his maternal grandfather had been rector at Elphin and master of the diocesan school there, while his paternal grandfather had married the dean of Elphin's daughter. This band of relatives, well-meaning, ready with practical help and advice, but sometimes interfering and overwatchful, provided a stable yet potentially oppressive environment. The impulsive and restless side of Goldsmith's nature must have found the family bonds uncomfortable, the closeness of the circle constricting. Yet the domestic pieties of that circle, its certitudes, the very uniformity of its daily routines, made it a point of emotional reference throughout his life. His letters from London in the late 1750s, when he was struggling to establish himself and to find a sense of direction, are full of a mildly envious longing for the "domestic tranquillity" of those who have given up ambition, those whose adventures consist of visiting neighbors and occasionally making "a migration from the blue bed to the brown." He writes to his cousin, Robert Bryanton: "Every day do I remember the calm anecdotes of your life, from the fire-side to the easy chair."[3] That "fire-side," standing for all domestic contentment, will reappear with significant frequency in Goldsmith's works.

Although these eighteenth-century Goldsmiths represented the established church, the Protestant religion of England imposed on the Catholic Irish, the family's roots would seem to have been nourished by a different faith and culture. Goldsmith himself spoke of being descended from one Juan Romero, a Spaniard who came over to England in the sixteenth or early seventeenth century. Having moved to Ireland and married a Miss Goldsmith, he took his wife's name, perhaps changing his religion at the same time.[4] This mysterious foreigner may be a partly fictionalized version of the poet's great-great-grandfather, who is known to have been originally a Catholic, and whose brother was a priest in Holland. Before his marriage and conversion he may also have been the loose-living friar among whose illegitimate offspring, according to later tradition, were the ancestors of the eighteenth-century Goldsmiths.[5] There was certainly a "romantic turn" in the family, as Goldsmith remarked, using the adjective in its then current sense of imprudent and impractical; his elder brother Henry married for love and had to leave the university without taking a degree, thereby consigning himself to the humblest stations in the church. Goldsmith goes on (he is in fact writing to Henry) to refer to a common streak of restlessness, a desire for fortune combined with an eagerness to squander it. He was himself a gambler throughout his life.[6]

The rector's house at Lissoy was a substantial, two-story building, standing at the end of an avenue of ash trees. Seventy acres of farmland went with the house; like the Vicar of Wakefield, Charles Goldsmith could augment his stipend with the proceeds of husbandry. The adjoining cottages would have been occupied by the farmworkers, among them the dairymaid whose melancholy ballads retained a favored place in Goldsmith's memory. He delighted in singing, whether invited to do so or not, "Barbara Allen," "Johnny Armstrong's Last Good Night," and "Death and the Lady."[7]

Goldsmith's sister remembered him as exhibiting in infancy the abrupt changes of mood that were to mark his whole life, alternations of shyness, reserve, and despondency with pleasant good humor and happy sociability. He was, she said, "remarkably humorous but it was uncommon." In the main he was too serious and reserved, "but when in Spirrits none more agreeably so." He was evidently in spirits on the occasion of a tea party at the rectory. Another small boy in the company, being asked to carry the kettle to the table, found its handle so warm that he hastily protected his fingers with the lap of his coat. As he did so, Catherine relates, "the Ladys perceived some thing which made them Laugh immodarately," and the seven-year-old Goldsmith was not slow to realize what had amused them. Knowing that his father, no puritan, would share the joke, Goldsmith reported the incident and was promised a reward of gingerbread if he could turn it into verse. The result perhaps owes its classical allusion and jokey rhymes to the abetting parent:

> Theseus did see, as Poets say,
> Dark Hell and its abysses,
> But had not half so Sharp an Eye
> As our young Charming Misses.
>
> For they could through boy's breeches peep,
> And view what ere he had there;
> It seemed to Blush, and they all Laughd
> Because the face was all Bare.
>
> They laughed at that which some times Else
> Might give them greatest pleasure.
> How quickly the[y] could see the thing
> Which was their darling treasure!

Not only are these verses precociously knowing; they could also claim to be the smuttiest lines that Goldsmith ever wrote.

Meanwhile his more formal education was not neglected. At the village school he came under the spell of Thomas Byrne, a retired soldier who was versed both in the classics and in Irish legends and folktales. Though he may have failed to instill much learning into the boy, whose fellow pupils, the sons of neighboring gentlemen, judged to be a "stupid, heavy blockhead, little better than a fool, whom every one made fun of,"[8] the schoolmaster touched his imagination with stories of foreign lands, and gave him, as his sister recalled, a taste for travel. She also believed that Byrne taught her brother to "feel more for every creature he saw in distress then for him self." In fact, generous feeling and tenderheartedness ran in the family and needed little prompting from Thomas Byrne. For Catherine suggests a close parallel between the character and circumstances of the Man in Black (*The Citizen of the World,* Letters 26 and 27) and those of his creator. The Man in Black's father, modeled on Charles Goldsmith, has unmistakably a "romantic turn," believing wholeheartedly and impractically in goodness of heart. His children have been taught "to consider all the wants of mankind as our own, to regard the *human face divine* with affection and esteem. He wound us up to be mere machines of pity [so that they responded like clockwork automata at the sight of misery], and rendered us incapable of withstanding the slightest impulse made either by real or fictitious distress."[9] Living among a population wretchedly poor, dressed in rags, and often starving, the Goldsmiths rarely lacked worthy recipients of charity. When he was a student at Trinity College Goldsmith was discovered one morning trying to free himself from the ticking and feathers of his mattress. He had given his blankets away to a woman with five children and a sick husband, and in an effort to keep warm had cut a hole in the mattress and crept inside.

By now Oliver was one of six children, and financial pressure compelled his parents to establish priorities. Henry, seven or eight years his senior, was destined for the university and, inevitably, the church. For Oliver, surprisingly, a career in business was decided on, and he was sent away to school. For a time he boarded with an uncle at Ballyoughter, where family and friends continued the idolizing that his relatives generally indulged in, treating him as a prodigy of learning and cleverness. The idolized young are often expected to show their paces. Goldsmith was "obliged" (the verb is Catherine's) to exercise his wit on various subjects, as he was obliged to submit to the trammels of education. Both kinds of pressure were irksome. The stupidity with which he confronted his official instructors looks like a dogged refusal to conform, a refusal to be forced into dependence and a kind of servitude. Significantly, the only teacher of whom Goldsmith ever spoke favorably, the Reverend Patrick Hughes, master of the Edgeworthstown school that Goldsmith attended from 1741 to 1745, treated his pupil like a friend, and "conversed with him on a footing very different from that of a young Scholar." For this granting of esteem and dignity, Hughes gained

Goldsmith's undying "gratitude and Respect."[10] Hughes created a congenial atmosphere, and from being awkward and diffident the boy became a
leader in his schoolfellows' sports and games, participating in pranks and
"scenes of humour" (he never lost his fondness for practical jokes), demonstrating his athleticism and high spirits. His friends also noted, however, the
sensitiveness of his temper: "easily offended, though easily appeased."[11]

The foundations of Goldsmith's excellent knowledge of French were perhaps laid at Edgeworthstown. Much time would have been occupied with
the classical languages, for this final period of schooling was the result of a
new assessment of his prospects, probably initiated, and to some extent financially guaranteed, by his uncle, Thomas Contarine. The new plan was to
prepare him for entry to Trinity College, Dublin, with an eye to a professional career. That this decision on behalf of the favorite child was not altogether popular emerges from Catherine's statement that "his father Chose
rather to distress his younger Children and encourage [Oliver's] Genius by
sending him to the College."

It was on his final journey from Lissoy to Edgeworthstown, for his last
term at school, that occurred what was to form the main action of *She Stoops
to Conquer*, or, as it was originally entitled (and later subtitled) *The Mistakes
of a Night*. The episode was appropriately memorialized in the theater, for
it shows Goldsmith dramatizing himself, playing the role of leisurely traveler and sightseer, and, as the victim of a hoax, becoming the unwitting
creator of a dramatic situation. He was riding to Edgeworthstown alone,
though a mere 13-year-old, and was determined to take his time. Beyond
Ballymahon he left the direct road, turning west to view the elegant country
houses in that part of County Longford. With a guinea in his pocket, he decided to prolong the agreeable time by putting up for the night in the village of Ardagh. He was actor enough to adopt the proper style, and firmly
asked a passerby for directions to "the best house in Town." By "house" he
meant inn, but unluckily he had addressed the local wag, who willfully
took the noun in its literal sense, and sent Goldsmith off to the finest residence in Ardagh. It was, like that in *She Stoops to Conquer*, a commodious
house that he could, and did, mistake for an inn. Knowing what was expected of practiced travelers, he ordered his horse to be well looked after,
and covered his nervousness by rushing into the most likely looking public
room, in fact a handsome and private parlor. And there was the apparent
landlord, sitting before a good fire. After the customary greetings Goldsmith boldly threw himself into the part: "I believe a bottle of wine could
not be bad this cold night. I have been fasting all day, and would be obliged
if you would get me something comfortably good in a hurry, for I am very

hungry." The landlord, in reality Sir George Fetherstone, began to suspect his guest's error, but being a man who enjoyed a joke, thought he would play the little comedy out. A meal was provided, host and guest sat together over a bottle, and were later joined by the "landlord's" wife and daughters. Rising magnificently to the occasion, Goldsmith called for two more bottles, insisting that the ladies should choose their own wine. Before retiring he took the seasoned traveler's precaution of bespeaking an early and adequate breakfast. Only when he called for his bill in the morning were the mistakes of the night laid bare, and Goldsmith surfeited on shame and confusion.[12] This raw material is most directly utilized in *She Stoops to Conquer*, but the emotional charge of the situation also fed the most amusing scene in Goldsmith's first comedy, *The Good-Natured Man*, which dramatizes the acute embarrassment of a young man attempting to entertain, simultaneously, his fiancée and the bailiffs. Comic heroes are frequently put into tight corners, or find themselves awkwardly caught by their own ingenuity, but a richly embarrassing situation, created by trick or error and blunderingly or blindly persevered in, is Goldsmith's special dramatic province.

In that summer of 1745 he was admitted to Trinity College as a sizar, or "poor scholar," on the lowest rung of a very clearly demarcated hierarchy. As a sizar he was in not merely a humble but a menial position, earning a reduction in fees by performing such duties as waiting on the fellows at table and sweeping floors. Fourteen years later the humiliation still rankled; in 1759 he wrote to Henry that a young man who has "ambition, strong passions, and an exquisite sensibility of contempt"—Goldsmith is obviously describing himself—would be well advised to keep away from Trinity College.[13] Trinity was not the republic of letters that Goldsmith might have expected, but a petty tyranny. In his *Inquiry into the Present State of Polite Learning in Europe*, published a few months after the letter to Henry, he reverts to the Trinity student's lot, with an emphasis now on the "absurd" pride of those in authority who demand to be waited on by the poor scholars, and on the injustice of the situation, which is also a perversion of logic and language: "It implies a contradiction, for men to be at once learning the *liberal* arts, and at the same time treated as *slaves*, at once studying freedom, and practicing servitude" (1:336; Goldsmith's italics). The hurtful experience must have powerfully reinforced his hatred of injustice; conversely, justice was to remain for him the one cardinal virtue. The manifest oppression of the university system also strengthened his desire for self-sufficiency and his concern with liberty.

Principal tyrant at the college was his tutor, Dr. Theaker Wilder, a man quick-tempered, aggressive, and cruel. Goldsmith complained to Percy that

Wilder "used him very harshly." Since mathematics was Wilder's special field, and an obligatory part of the curriculum, it did not help matters that Goldsmith held the subject in contempt.[14] The jibe in the *Inquiry*, that mathematics "seems a science to which the meanest intellects are equal" (1:335), looks like revenge on the brutal Wilder. Goldsmith was happy only in his classical studies, where he gained official commendations and the tributes of his contemporaries, who long remembered the skill and elegance of his translations. Their admiration soothed his hurt pride, while his tutor's harassment could be forgotten in social gatherings. Thanks to his good humor when in agreeable company, Goldsmith was popular. He was invited to parties, and himself arranged a dance and supper in his room. Both sexes were invited, in blatant breach of college rules. Unfortunately (but Goldsmith was rarely fortunate) the project, or the din it created, came to Dr. Wilder's ears. He burst in, abused, and finally struck his student—a blow that was never forgotten or forgiven.

Goldsmith did not wait to receive a formal admonition. With characteristic impetuosity he simply walked out of the college. With equally characteristic reluctance to leave a place where there were sights to be seen and easy companions to be with, he lingered in Dublin until he had spent all but a shilling. He then set out for Cork, intending to walk the 130 miles, and thence betake himself to North America. By the time he had tramped 80 of those miles his funds and his footwear were exhausted. A handful of gray peas, given him by a girl at a country fair, seemed to him, as he later told his sister, "the most Comfortable repast he ever made." "He then to Late began to think of what he had done, and as the Prod[i]gal son returned to his father after suffering all that nakedness and famine could endure." His sister may well be accurate in implying that her chameleon-like brother was once again casting himself in a role, this time as the prodigal son making his sorrowful return.

His brother Henry effected a reconciliation with the college authorities. Their father, who died early in 1747, was perhaps already too ill to travel to Dublin for that purpose. At his death the family was left penurious, but with Contarine's financial help and the gaining of a college award, Goldsmith was able to continue his studies, though the end of his undergraduate career was muddled and unsatisfactory. In May 1747 he helped to rescue a student who had been arrested for debt. The offending bailiff was collared and soused beneath the college pump. (The episode has historical importance, as the first recorded confrontation between Goldsmith and a bailiff.) The emboldened students marched on the city jail in a liberating mood, only to be halted by the military. Expulsions and reprimands followed.

Goldsmith was merely rebuked, having with customary candor made a frank and disarming confession of his guilt. But he seems to have suffered suspension on academic grounds later in the year, and to have retired to Contarine's home to complete his studies in private. He returned to Dublin in February 1750 to be formally admitted to the degree of B.A., having extended his course eight months beyond the statutory four years.

Goldsmith told Thomas Percy that immediately after graduating he began his medical studies (presumably also at Trinity) "and took the Degree of M.B. when he was about 20." No evidence has been found to support this claim, and his sister tells a very different story. Goldsmith's memory may have slipped. More probably his statement was a complete fabrication, for though he certainly went to Edinburgh in 1752 to study medicine, and from Edinburgh to Leiden, there is a total lack of proof that he obtained a medical degree from any European university. When he talked to Percy he had gone too far to retreat. By 1773 he had had brief spells of medical practice, was widely known as "Dr. Goldsmith," and had claimed (verbally) to be a bachelor of physic of Dublin when the University of Oxford honored him with an *ad eundem gradum* degree in 1769. He may have supplicated for a medical qualification in the 1750s on the strength of his studies in Edinburgh; he comments in the *Inquiry* that that university will grant a license to practice a profession "when the student thinks proper" (1:333). Or he may have believed that his studies sufficiently qualified him without the need for a stamp of official approval.

His sister's account of the two years between Dublin and Edinburgh tells of drifting uncertainty. Thomas Contarine, playing a paternal part, tried to direct his nephew into the church. Goldsmith's reluctance in yielding to pressure did not escape Catherine's notice. She recalled that he "never liked" this enforced submission to another's will and dependence on another's purse. He wished to be free, and his restless nature craved change of occupation and of place. Not an enthusiastic candidate for holy orders, he was predictably rejected. He then spent time with his mother, who had moved into a smaller house in Ballymahon, running errands for her. If Catherine is right in calling him his mother's "greatest favourite," she may have been glad to have him about the house. Eventually the tireless Contarine secured him an appointment as resident tutor in a gentleman's family. A position of servitude and constraint could not suit Goldsmith for long—his sister's refrain is that "he never liked confinement"—and he left after a year.

The idea of emigrating, or at least of escaping from the family circle, drove him to ride off to Cork, on a good horse and with £30 in his pocket. In his travels, as in other things, Goldsmith was always in extremes, either well set up and showily affluent, or impecunious and half-starved. Six weeks later he was back in Ballymahon in the latter condition, having spent or gambled away his money, and having exchanged his horse for a wretched nag. His mother insisted on a full explanation, a coercion that Goldsmith evaded by unfolding a wonderful yarn. He had sold his horse in Cork to buy his passage to North America. Three weeks had gone by, waiting for a favorable wind, while he followed his favorite pursuit, seeing "every thing curious in and about the City." When the wind finally changed he just happened to be on a country excursion, and so missed his boat. After purchasing his new, scraggy, horse, he was left with five shillings; that, as he thoughtfully admitted (no doubt with the mildly solemn frown caught in the Reynolds portrait) "was rather little" to cover the return journey. A call on a former college friend, who had often promised hospitality, turned into a comic disaster, since his host proved to be mean and grudging. Goldsmith was saved by the arrival of a more courteous and openhanded neighbor. The ensuing scene, with the false friend eulogizing the worthy Goldsmith, while the latter walks to and fro, biting his lip and looking daggers, is a fine piece of dramatic elaboration—or invention. Happily the polite neighbor takes Goldsmith home with him for a few days, where he plays bowls with the daughters of the house, and listens to them singing to the harpsichord while their father weeps at the memory of his late wife.

Catherine, in retelling this story of a "foolish ramble," is probably recording, as Katharine Balderston suggests, her brother's first piece of fiction.[15] One detail—that his mean friend offered to loan him a horse but produced instead an oak walkingstick—almost certainly derives from Isaac Walton's biography of Richard Hooker, and reappears in *The Vicar of Wakefield*. Like much of Goldsmith's later work, the tale has something for every taste: sentimental pathos, cynicism, understated wit, farcical comedy, and self-mockery. That it had some basis in fact is indicated by his later assuring Catherine of its veracity, which may only mean that the elaborate embroidery conceals a slender outline of fact. At the time, overwhelmed by the recriminations of the assembled family, Goldsmith took the line of least resistance and admitted that there was not a word of truth in the whole story. He must have felt that he had suffered enough, that the family had not given the prodigal the welcome that it was in duty bound to give. Most revealing is his touchingly desperate plea: "And now Dear Mother . . . since I have struggeld so hard to come home to you, why are you not better pleased to see me?" The appeal was met only by an austere reminder of his obligations: had he written a thank-you letter to his hospitable acquaintance? The once-favorite child had tried his mother's patience too far. He must have asked himself whether he was so palpably being denied affection because he deserved none; perhaps there was no good reason why his mother should be pleased to see him. But if his affections were to be thus repulsed, he could—the spoilt child becoming truculent—repudiate in his turn. Once he had left Ireland he seems never to have written to his mother, and his inquiries about her are cool. When she died in 1770 he wore only half-mourning, and shocked Reynolds's sister by explaining that he had lost "only a distant relation."[16] The pun was bitterly accurate.

In the aimless days that followed, when he "did not know well what to do with himself," he fished, walked, and played the flute, on which he is said to have been a competent performer, but which he sometimes used simply to relieve his feelings. He went "visiting about among his friends," drinking with cronies in Conway's inn at Ballymahon or in The Pigeons at Lissoy, experiences that would be turned to account in creating Tony Lumpkin and his drinking companions.[17]

Contarine's patience was inexhaustible. The legal profession was a possibility, and Goldsmith's name was entered at the Temple Inn, London. Though he would be briefly resident in the Temple a few years later, and again for the last seven years of his life, he was not destined to arrive there just yet. Having reached Dublin he proceeded to gamble away the funds that Contarine had supplied. With comic inevitability he had once more journeyed to the borders of his native land, and once more had failed to leave it. He was to write later of that "Unaccountable fondness for country, this maladie du Pays, as the french call it," and to confess to this fondness even though he had received nothing but "civil contempt" while living in Ireland. The magnetism of his native land was powerful. Yet once he had broken away, and had decided to make his home in the literary capital of Great Britain, it was impossible ever to return. He writes with vague promises of intended visits. He compares the view from Greenwich Hill, to its disadvantage, with that from "the little mount before Lishoy gate," which yields "the most pleasing horizon in nature." He compares his uncertain existence in London with Henry's peaceful, unassuming curate's establishment at Kilkenny, happy "among your own children or those who knew you as a child." But he cannot go back, partly because by returning he would subject his hard-earned and still precarious identity as a writer, his only identity, to contempt: "whatever airs I may give myself on this side of the water, my dignity I fancy would be evaporated before I reach'd the other. I know you have in Ireland a very indifferent Idea of a man who writes for bread." Perhaps even more important, some of the sources of his writing would also evaporate if he crossed the water. He fears that all may have changed in Ireland, and changed for the worse: "I suppose before I return I shall find all the blooming virgins I once left in Westmeath shrivelled into a parcel of hags with seven children a piece tearing down their petticoats." The chronological confusion—"before I return I shall find"—betrays an emotional confusion. He needs to think, or rather to feel, that all is the same, that the Ireland he knew is unmarked by time, a ground upon which his memories and imagination can securely rest. Although Auburn, the deserted village, has ostensibly been depopulated to enlarge the parkland of some great landowner, the result, as Goldsmith's poem presents it, is in fact a countryside reduced to its original uncultivated state. The landscape, which purports to be that surrounding an English village, now strongly resembles, in its fauna and flora—bittern, lapwing, sedges, cresses, long grass, furze—the fenny shores of Lough Ree, the "plashy" or marshy springs, the islands "surrounded with sedgy moors," where Goldsmith had wandered as a boy. Nostalgic reminiscence, the "unaccountable fondness" for a countryside charged with the dearest memories, has blurred the logic of the poem's argument.[18]

Whether he was now trapped at home as a result of fecklessness, or because of some deeper compulsion, he was reduced, in his sister's words, to the condition of a "hart-broken dejected being." The family reconvened to determine his future. Two professions remained. No one seems to have thought of the army, though Goldsmith was athletic and well-built. Instead his anxious family propelled him into medicine. Edinburgh University, probably the best medical school in Europe, was selected for his training, and in the autumn of 1752, in his early twenties, Goldsmith finally broke the bonds of country and family.

His first near mishap in Edinburgh was perfectly in character. Having found lodgings and deposited his luggage he set out, ever inquisitive, to inspect the city. Too late he realized that in his usual hurry he had forgotten to note down his new address. Wandering among the narrow streets he providentially encountered the very porter who had carried his portmanteau. Once settled he carefully portrayed himself in his letters to Ireland as a serious student, reading into the night and attending lectures. He particularly admired those of Professor Alexander Monro, whom he judged both "a skilfull Physician" and "an able Orator" with a real gift for exposition.[19] Monro perhaps served as an early model for Goldsmith, no mean expositor himself in matters scientific and historical. What Goldsmith did not advertise was his enrolling in the Edinburgh Medical Society (a student club), and his moving into lodgings with other students, whom he entertained with songs and stories, and amused by his sartorial extravagance. Some of his tailor's bills have survived. The items—including "rich Sky-Blew sattin," fine worsted hose, a quantity of superfine "high Clarett-colour'd Cloth"—do not suggest penny-pinching.[20] He gave pleasure the rein, perhaps somewhat in the manner of his great-great-grandfather; Percy's biography hints that he injured his health during this period by bouts of dissipation.[21]

In the 1750s Edinburgh also offered more sober enjoyments. There was music making and dancing. Goldsmith, with his delight in observing as well as participating in social pleasures, and with his interest (to blossom in the biography of Beau Nash) in the conducting and regulating of such entertainments, attended and duly reported:

when a stranger enters the danceing-hall he sees one end of the room taken up by the Lady's, who sit dismally in a Groupe by themselves. On the other end stand their pensive partners, that are to be. . . . the Ladies indeed may ogle, and the Gentlemen sigh, but an embargo is laid on any closer commerce; at length . . . the Lady directeress . . . pitches on a Gentleman and Lady to walk a minuet, which they perform with a formality that approaches despondence. After five or six couple have thus walked the Gauntlett, all stand up to country dance's . . . so they dance much, say nothing, and thus concludes our assembly.[22]

Other Edinburgh doors were open to him. He received a brief schooling in scandal among a party of ladies, but he is too honest to pretend that, where female company is concerned, he is anything but an outsider. "An ugly and a poor man is society only for himself and such society the world lets me enjoy in great abundance." So he may "sit down and laugh at the world, and at myself—the most ridiculous object in it."[23] The pain behind the forced jocularity is clear, and clearly that of the would-be participant who is restricted to the role of detached spectator. It is the pain of the exile.

If it is wretched to be on the outside, it is worse to be accepted only in order to be used and exploited. During the winter of 1753 Goldsmith spent several days at the young duke of Hamilton's, flattered by the dinner invitations, endeavoring to be the informal companion, naively letting the company into his "circumstances and manner of thinking," only to realize that he was liked "more as a *jester* than as a companion." He had been typecast as "the facetious Irish man," so that he could be patronized and treated with an indulgence bordering on contempt. We know how Goldsmith responded to contempt. He told his uncle how, when the painful truth dawned, he had stood on his personal dignity—"I disdained so servile an employment"—and on the dignity of his métier: " 'twas unworthy my calling as a physician."[24]

Once out of Ireland, Goldsmith could move yet further away. Still financially dependent on his uncle, he announced to him his plans to continue his medical studies in Paris. Early in 1754 he set out. He may have had Paris in mind, but in fact he arrived in Leiden, an important center of medical education though no longer as prestigious as it had been under Boerhaave. The journey was interrupted by a short period in an English jail. It is not clear whether debt collectors had pursued him from Edinburgh; whether he had unwisely stood bail for a friend; or whether he was suspected of being, as some of his fellow passengers really were, in the pay of the French king. Having disembarked in Rotterdam he went on to Leiden through a countryside more attractive, because more like central Ireland, than the surroundings of Edinburgh. Finding that travel in Holland was inexpensive, he indulged his taste, reporting to Contarine that the Dutch "sail in coverd boats drawn by horses and in these you are sure to meet people of all nations. . . . any man who likes company may have them to his Taste." Here too, however, as in Edinburgh, he was often the outsider: "I generally detachd myself from all society and was wholy Taken up in observing the face of the country."[25]

After approximately a year's residence in Leiden, Goldsmith was on the move again. He had already informed his uncle that a period of study in Paris would present no difficulties since he was "perfectly acquainted" with the language. His easy familiarity with French is attested both by his writings, some of them direct translations, others borrowing from and adapting French sources, and by his bookshelves: when his library was posthumously auctioned the catalog listed numerous French works of travel, bibliography, and natural history, besides the expected literary classics.[26] Perhaps, like George Primrose in *The Vicar of Wakefield*, Goldsmith planned to visit Paris "with no design but just to look about [him], and then to go forward" (4:118). Like George, he walked from Holland to Paris; both of them were doing what the Danish writer and traveler Ludvig Holberg had done at the beginning of the century. James Prior first drew attention to Goldsmith's admiration for the recently deceased Holberg. It is a plausible conjecture that Goldsmith was modeling himself on a man who from humble beginnings had risen to great fame, and who had determined to experience Europe by making the Grand Tour as a pedestrian. In the *Inquiry into Polite Learning* Goldsmith cites Holberg's journeyings as a signal instance of resourcefulness and independence: "he travelled by day, and at night sung at the doors of peasants' houses to get himself a lodging." Holberg provided a precedent to follow, and an identity to adopt: that of the unorthodox sightseer.[27].

With minimal luggage—a single clean shirt and his flute—Goldsmith passed through Flanders and northern France to Paris. There he may have pursued in a desultory fashion his medical education (he attended lectures on chemistry), and more systematically his education in life. He visited the theater and walked the streets, lamenting the visible hunger and subjection of the poor. After Paris he moved on to Strasbourg, then to Germany and Switzerland. It may be that from Paris to Geneva he was engaged as a tutor to a young Englishman, and that he therefore went by coach. In the *Inquiry* he notes that "A man who is whirled through Europe in a post-chaise, and the pilgrim who walks the Grand Tour on foot, will form very different conclusions. *Haud inexpertus loquor* [I speak from experience]" (1:331). Those who go by coach are above their fellow men; the foot traveler is on a level with them. Moreover, he is a "pilgrim," a *peregrinus*, a traveling stranger, more humble, certainly more exposed to insult than other classes of voyager.

The summer of 1755 found Goldsmith moving through the Alps toward Italy, and already planning "The Traveller," the poem that nine years later would decisively establish his name. Padua detained him for six months, followed by Verona and Venice. Then, toward the end of the year, he began his homeward trek, supporting himself in Holberg's manner by begging a night's accommodation in exchange for a tune on the flute, or a song; Goldsmith had a good ear, and sang with much feeling. He may have tried to augment his funds by gambling, or by asking for loans. He confessed to his brother-in-law in 1757 that "there is hardly a Kingdom in Europe in which I am not a debtor,"[28] and his early essays, as Ralph Wardle points out, reveal an intimate knowledge of the art of living on credit, and of the rebuffs and excuses that meet the man who tries to borrow money.[29] Some continental universities offered prizes to visiting disputants, and Goldsmith seems to have entered these combats. Though he cuts a meager figure in most of the discussions that Boswell records, he could acquit himself well in other companies. When settled in London he joined one of the most vigorous, and some would say dangerously freethinking, debating clubs, the Robin Hood Society, where moral, social, political, and religious topics were examined. Though not a frequent attender at the weekly meetings, he commanded respect as "a good Orator, and a candid Disputant," where "candid" implies both warmth of feeling and sincerity.[30]

Early in 1756 Goldsmith landed at Dover. A year later he was to learn that his long-suffering family had attempted to transmit money to him in Padua. He now knew only that his letters from abroad had gone unanswered. He felt himself at best forgotten, at worst disowned: "no soul cares a farthing about me."[31] Rather than appeal for help, he determined to seek a living in London. His enemy now was English insularity; he later claimed that the deep prejudice of Londoners against the Irish—his brogue immediately identified him—kept him unemployed. Eventually he was engaged as an apothecary's assistant in the City, and was subsequently encouraged to set up as a physician in Bankside. He was working among the poor and deprived, perhaps even living among beggars, and was brought up sharply against urban poverty and squalor. There were patients, but few fees. Given his impulsively generous nature, he probably did not charge enough, or was too softhearted to enforce payment for his services. Being "Doctor Goldsmith" gave him at least a satisfying identity, and opportunities to indulge his benevolent and humane instincts. But maintaining status called for ingenuity. His secondhand velvet coat was prominently patched; the doctor saved appearances by carefully holding his hat to his chest during consultations.

At some point he tried to interest Samuel Richardson, printer as well as novelist, in an embryonic tragedy. He clearly did not yet see which way his literary bent would take him. Meanwhile a friend from Edinburgh days invited Goldsmith to become acting head of his father's school at Peckham, then a village on the outskirts of London. The headmaster's daughter remembered Goldsmith as being "remarkably cheerful," treating his pupils to sweets, joining in boyish pranks, and organizing practical jokes.[32] This lightheartedness may to some extent have been assumed, a mask to hide unhappiness, for, according to William Cooke, Goldsmith was always pained by recalling his days at Peckham as a time of particular humiliation.[33] (He might have found it amusing that Peckham, no longer a village, commemorates him by way of the Oliver Goldsmith Infant School.) There seems to have been a further period of employment as usher or junior teacher, and if this was also at Peckham it might explain the contradictory evidence. What appears certain is that it is Goldsmith's own tribulations that are recalled in the essay "On Education," where the usher is depicted as the laughingstock of the entire school: "the oddity of his manners, his dress, or his language [the Irish brogue?] are a fund of eternal ridicule"; he is little better than a slave.[34] Servitude and contempt: the usher's lot is composed of what Goldsmith most hates and fears.

After two and a half years in London he was far from being settled. Then in the autumn of 1758 all seemed changed. He was appointed, or perhaps only promised an appointment, as civilian physician to the East India Company, to serve on the Coromandel coast, with a yearly salary of £1,000.[35]

Here was the opportunity to see more of the world, and to be somebody in the world. Ironically, the appointment brought yet another humiliation. In order to earn his passage money, Goldsmith offered himself as a hospital mate. At the interview his medical knowledge was found to be inadequate, and he was turned down. The board's decision was a wise one. When he briefly took up medicine again, in the summer of 1765, an apothecary declined to prepare one of his prescriptions, fearing it might harm the patient.

Amidst these false starts Goldsmith's real career had been accidentally launched. The Peckham headmaster introduced him to Ralph Griffiths, proprietor of the *Monthly Review*, who saw the advantage of having on his staff a widely traveled and well-read young man, trained in both classics and medicine. Goldsmith's fluency in French was a particular recommendation; one of his first contributions to the journal was a translation, with minor additions, of a long item from a French periodical. Soon he had contracted with Griffiths and another publisher to translate Jean Marteilhe's *Mémoires d'un Protestant*, a history of persecution and suffering that would have appealed to someone of Goldsmith's sensibilities.

Reviewing for Griffiths lasted only from April to September 1757, for the conditions under which he worked were irksome. Griffiths and his wife did what no young writer can tolerate: they rewrote his text. Soon, however, the *Memoirs of a Protestant* was in print (March 1758), and he had additionally contracted to produce a biography of Voltaire. He also planned to capitalize on his firsthand experience of European culture with a compact but ambitiously titled work, *An Inquiry into the Present State of Polite Learning in Europe*. And early in 1759 he was contributing to Smollett's *Critical Review*, the *Monthly*'s great rival. So that when, in March of that year, he finally had to abandon the East India scheme, since hostilities between English and French forces made the area unsafe, he was well on the way to becoming a man of letters. What had begun as a financial stopgap was now to be his livelihood. For the next 15 years, apart from one brief medical interlude, he was committed to literature.

When his relatively short literary career came to an end, Goldsmith had proved himself as poet, essayist, novelist, historian, biographer, and dramatist, a genuinely miscellaneous writer of great versatility, fully deserving Johnson's well-known praise: "he adorned every kind of writing that he touched."[36] He had been sought out by established and aspiring authors, had been an intimate friend of Sir Joshua Reynolds, the most renowned portrait painter of his day, and had been one of the nine original members of

The Club, eighteenth-century London's most famous and most exclusive intellectual group.

One would expect that as his fame accrued, as his status as professional writer grew more assured, so he would personally grow more assured, more secure in himself. The signs are otherwise, though the symptoms were often exaggerated and misinterpreted. Everyone agreed, for instance, that he was absurdly extravagant and ridiculously vain. The furnishings of his rooms in the Temple included four blue moreen window curtains, one of them an elaborate festoon, with a mahogany sofa and dining chairs upholstered in the same expensive fabric. These seemed designed to announce proudly to visitors that Goldsmith had attained the "genteel independance for life" that he had set himself to acquire.[37] They were in actuality rather hollow witnesses, for the splendor had contributed to the debts, estimated at £2,000, that Goldsmith left behind him, and that elicited Johnson's wondering question: "Was ever poet so trusted before?"[38] The splendor was also evident in Goldsmith's notoriously showy dress. Other tailors' bills, besides those from Edinburgh, have survived; Goldsmith never lost his taste for rich embroidered waistcoats and blue silk breeches. Boswell records an episode at his lodgings in October 1769, when "to divert the tedious minutes" while waiting for a late dinner guest, Goldsmith "strutted about, bragging of his dress." Boswell points to a double motive. Goldsmith is transparently, and therefore harmlessly, boasting of his fine attire, but he is equally harmlessly amusing the company, literally "diverting" it by leading its impatience into different and more cheerful channels. Though his behavior on this occasion drew insults—Garrick hinted that he was the worst-dressed gentleman he knew; Johnson said outright that Goldsmith's coat was of an absurd color—it also drew attention to himself.[39] He was for a time the center of the circle, was being seen, was unmistakably identifiable. Hence the importance of being "Doctor Goldsmith," for the eighteenth-century physician had a distinctive uniform: scarlet greatcoat, large wig, gold-headed cane, and sword. Thus dressed for the part, Goldsmith walked abroad as a professional man, even if not a practicing one, and even if the result struck some bystanders as ludicrous: "Look at that fly with a long pin stuck through it."[40] Earlier, in picturing himself as a medical student, Goldsmith had self-consciously seen himself in that role, with his books, his anatomical skeleton, and his cat. Likewise, he had comically portrayed himself as a sightseer, ambling off to view the Highlands on a donkey the size of a ram. In London in 1758 he had been the typical Grub Street hack, writing in a garret for his bread, and expecting to be dunned by his landlady for failing to pay his milk bill.[41]

In so describing himself Goldsmith seems to be alluding to Hogarth's picture of *The Distressed Poet*. In his search for an identity Goldsmith modeled himself on others, most strenuously when he was beginning to be known as a writer. According to Boswell, more than one observer shared his opinion that Goldsmith "studiously copied" Johnson's conversational manner. Joseph Warton, whose stumbling syntax testifies to the difficulty of assessing his subject, declared: "Of all solemn coxcombs, Goldsmith is the first; yet sensible—but affects to use Johnson's hard words in conversation." Reynolds, who knew him best, saw that his uneasiness about being admitted into the polite world led him to cast about "furiously" for patterns of behavior: "For one week he took one [person] for a model and for another week another."[42] His ability as a mimic, his gift for capturing other people's linguistic habits, which he may have cultivated precisely because he was unsure of himself, is fully displayed in the anecdote about a cobbler and a bailiff (recorded by Reynolds) that Goldsmith once related in order to prove that he could "tell a story as well as Mr. Garrick." The manner of telling is remarkably similar to that of Beau Nash, whose favorite story of a covetous old parson is reported in full in Goldsmith's biography. There is the same digressiveness and the same ostentation: "I entertained him," says Nash, "at my house in John's Court—no, my house in John's Court was not built then"; "Why," says Goldsmith, "the very best company used to come in our house. Squire Thomson used to dine with us, who was one of the first men in the country." Goldsmith also recollected Nash's habit of ineptly anticipating his audience's reaction: "I'll tell you something to that purpose, that I fancy will make you laugh"—a sure way of dampening amusement. Goldsmith improves on that, with calculated banality: "There lived a cobbler— some people do laugh at this story and some do not." Neither that bit of foolery, nor the deliberate inadequacies of his anecdote, seem to have been appreciated by his hearers, Reynolds included. Goldsmith had simply once again demonstrated his social clumsiness by his long and rambling story, and his unquenchable desire to shine by setting himself up in competition with Garrick.[43]

Reynolds recognized that the "horror which [Goldsmith] entertained of being overlooked by the company" prompted him to acts of buffoonery. In order to gather attention to himself, he would "sing, stand upon his head, or dance about the room."[44] He even risked reverting to the role of "facetious Irish man" in which he had been cast at the duke of Hamilton's, for according to William Cooke he rather cultivated his Irish brogue than endeavored to get rid of it.[45] From the same motive came those extravagant, unsupported assertions, those dogmatic judgments and unconvincing paradoxes that Boswell is pleased to set down, since they gave Johnson scope for ample and usually complete rebuttal. Goldsmith needed to be seen and heard, to be in every sense recognized; being overlooked and neglected meant losing one's identity and one's being.

But even worse than becoming invisible is becoming liable to scorn and insult, through being in some way deficient, unformed, incomplete. Metaphorically, this is the situation of the author whose works are excerpted and "epitomised" in newspaper reviews, becoming thereby "so mutilated as to render him contemptible" (1:505). This lurking fear of damage to his identity may account for the high incidence of physical mutilation, dismemberment, and deformity in Goldsmith's writings. The most startling and significant example occurs in the preface to the *Essays* of 1765. Goldsmith explains that he is reprinting his own pieces because he is impatient of unacknowledged borrowings from his work, of piracy, indeed of cannibalism: "I would desire . . . to imitate the fat man who I have somewhere read of in a shipwreck, who, when the sailors, pressed by famine, were taking slices from his posteriors to satisfy their hunger, insisted, with great justice, on having the first cut for himself" (3:2). The most bizarre instance is the threat to slice and devour the pearl fisher caught by the golden bait of the princess's daughters (2:358). A disgruntled author is advised to announce that he will eat up his own nose, by subscription, whereas a certain pregnant woman merely "long'd for a piece of her husband's nose."[46] The hardy veteran who bewails the death of the Princess Dowager of Wales is a rather extreme case: "Scarred, mangled, maimed in every part,/ Lopped of his limbs in many a gallant fight,/ In nought entire—except his heart" ("Threnodia Augustalis", ll.208–10; *Works*, 4:338). But there are many others who lose limbs in battle, in accidents, or even by legal process (2:110, 192, 266, 459; 3:104), while the rambling story that Reynolds records ends with the cobbler chopping off one of the bailiff's fingers. The dead are not immune, for an author can suffer posthumous desecration at the hands of critics. The somnambulist Cyrillo Padovano mangles a lady's corpse (3:217), a Chinese widow prepares to extract her late husband's heart (2:79), and Letter 85 of *The Citizen of the World* concludes with an image of a corpse "whose brains the embalmers have picked out through its ears." People are disfigured by smallpox, or goiter, or their vices; they are crippled or deaf, or exceptionally both deaf and dumb. Or they are mutilated in effigy: Beau Tibbs's room has for ornaments a "broken shepherdess" and a headless mandarin (2:231). It is not surprising that Goldsmith was irritated by Johnson's habit of abbreviating his friends' names: "I have often desired him not to call me *Goldy*."[47]

The other threat to his sense of achievement, and therefore to his sense of being, came from others' achievements. Their ascendance was a slighting of his own importance. Reynolds, who tried hard and sympathetically to resolve the anomalies that everyone could see in Goldsmith, confessed that his envy was his most unlikeable trait, the unacceptable face of his insecurity: "Goldsmith . . . considered fame as one great parcel, to the whole of which he laid claim, and whoever partook of any part of it, whether dancer, singer, slight of hand man, or tumbler, deprived him of his right, and drew off the attention of the world from himself, and which he was striving to gain."[48] At least Goldsmith made no secret of his feelings. He believed that all human beings are naturally vain and envious, and that it was better to admit these propensities than to let them smolder concealed.

As Reynolds also perceived, the desire for fame was at odds with Goldsmith's "sociable disposition." If he wished to be recognized, he also wished to be liked. Deliberately, therefore, he abandoned "his respectable character as a writer," throwing aside dignity and formality, and presented himself as a person to whom everyone, including "the ignorant and illiterate," could feel equal or even superior. "This," says Reynolds, "was his general principle"—but Goldsmith was trapped between contradictory impulses: "at times, observing the attention paid to the conversation of others who spoke with more premeditation, and the neglect of himself though greedy and impatient to speak, he then resolved to be more formal and to carry his character about with him. But as he found he could not unite both, he naturally relaxed into his old manner."[49] Even when he attempted to unite both characters in fiction, by making the sociable Mr. Burchell and the dignified and famous Sir William Thornhill one and the same person, the result is not wholly satisfactory.

The most remarkable absentees from Goldsmith's library shelves, according to the auctioneer's catalog, are his own publications. The catalog lists only an imperfect set, presumably an advance or proof copy, of his last major work, the *History of the Earth and Animated Nature*. A truly vain man would have done better than that. Goldsmith was a modest and basically shy person, yet one whose need for recognition continually pushed him into the limelight, with all its attendant anxieties: "There is not, perhaps, a more whimsically dismal figure in nature than a man of real modesty who assumes an air of impudence; who, while his heart beats with anxiety, studies ease and affects good humor. In this situation, however, a periodical writer often finds himself upon his first attempt to address the public in form. . . . Impressed with the terrors of the tribunal before which he is going to appear, his natural humor turns to pertness, and for real wit he is obliged to substitute vivacity" (1:353). Such is the opening paragraph of Goldsmith's periodical the *Bee* (1759). It expresses perfectly his own social dilemma, the anxious self-consciousness of the figure he cuts. Yet it reminds us that the literary self, the writer as he presents himself to his readers, is also an "assumed" being, that in the process of composition distortions and displacements occur. Goldsmith the man and Goldsmith the author may both play roles, and may play them from similar motives, but we must beware of treating the roles as identical.

Chapter Two
Learning the Trade

Exercising Judgment

It was of great benefit to Goldsmith that he began his literary career as a reviewer. His monthly stint for Ralph Griffiths included moral, historical, scientific, and philosophical works, and with these it was necessary to summarize and abridge, to evaluate the logical conduct of an argument, or to expose its lack of logic. There were plentiful opportunities for the sharpening of his faculties. When he was allocated works of literature, he could also sharpen the cutting edge of his prose. Sometimes his targets were extremely soft, like the fatuous romance *The Mother-in-Law, or the Innocent Sufferer*, whose pair of "lovyers" (Goldsmith mocks them with a jocular vulgarism) survive strange vicissitudes of fortune to end up happily wallowing in riches (1:82). Sometimes he applies a rather facile smartness to his victims, or borrows a manner of ironic scorn from Pope's *Art of Sinking in Poetry*, as in his strictures on Stephen Barrett's translation of Ovid (1:154–62).

Most important, throughout this apprenticeship Goldsmith is evolving his critical principles. His aversions are becoming clear: romances, because they offer deceptive, illusory images of human felicity (a view he shares with Johnson); undue reliance on epithets, because, like other "trifling ornaments," they dissipate the required strength of expression. These dislikes remain constant. Gray's *Elegy* is included in Goldsmith's anthology *The Beauties of English Poesy* (1767), but the reader is advised that although the poem is very fine, the lines are "overloaded with epithet" (5:320). And Goldsmith never succeeded in coming to terms with Shakespeare, whose "overcharged characters," "monsters and mummery" seemed too close to the excesses of romance (4:96; 1:189). Wildness and extravagance, "luxuriant images," turbulence and frenzy were anathema to Goldsmith's fastidious taste.

He has a keen eye for authorial vanity, and hence for affectation. An aspiring writer, encouraged by the flattering applause of his acquaintances, will affect a superiority he does not possess (1:14), showing off his learning by slavish imitation of classical structures, or by using blank verse, which always seemed to Goldsmith a pedantic vote in favor of classical, unrhymed forms. Or he asserts his uniqueness by silly coinages—"acrity," "machinal" (1:181), the "museful powers," in plain English the Muses (1:231)—or by abandoning propriety for a daring mixture of styles that is merely vulgar. So the author of *The Impetuous Lover, or, The Guiltless Parricide* (the italics are the reviewer's): "No sooner *would he* have repeated the name, and thereby recalled before his eyes the *lovely she*, than the whole *flux* of his imagination *bending* again to his beloved Iris, he would condemn his very suspicions as *foundationless*" (1:16). This reminds us of Ben Jonson's attack in *The Poetaster* on Marston's flatulent diction. Goldsmith's dislikes are Jonson's: pomposity, obscurity of utterance, affectation of language. He offered his *Beauties of English Poesy* to the public as a "useful, unaffected compilation."

From these negatives his positive principles may be deduced. The great virtue is to be natural, and therefore simple. The *Inquiry* makes his position quite explicit: "Let us, instead of writing finely, try to write naturally," a plea that, in its simplicity of utterance, fulfills itself (1:322). There is virtue also in consistency, though at the same time there is need for variety; consistency should not mean dullness. Modern tragedy has an advantage over Greek drama in point of "greater variety of passion and character" (1:223), and where passion is properly called for, it must be properly, that is powerfully, expressed. The poet working in epic or tragic genres must be able to "seize our passions in the strongest manner" (1:223), so as to get "within the soul" of his audience (1:173). According to Goldsmith's Chinese Philosopher, poetical merit lies in "glowing sentiment" and "striking imagery" (2:171), and one argument for rhyme as against blank verse is that the discipline of rhyming actually "lifts and increases the vehemence of every sentiment" (1:318). Another is that blank verse encourages floridness and prolixity; Goldsmith finds Thomson "in general a verbose and affected poet" (5:325). Writers in verse and prose should aim at what the Chinese Philosopher calls "conciseness of expression." This is neither simply an aesthetic absolute, nor a shrewd admission that some readers have low thresholds of boredom. The ethical and psychological basis of verbal concision emerges in Goldsmith's account of Samuel Butler, "the most modest man" among English poets. His personality led him to "avoid repetition or explanation" as an arrogant insult to the reader's intelligence, or "a tax upon his patience" that the author had no right to impose. The density of Butler's writings, both prose and verse, leaving "no interstice in the composition void of sentiment, nor even allow[ing] a pause for admiration," is the natural expression of the man's character (1:207–8). By the same token, Goldsmith's own

economy of expression signals the same qualities of personal modesty and
respect for his readers.

Prolixity is a particular snare for the comic writer, whose art is the most
demanding of all: "There is nothing in the whole province of writing more
difficult to attain than humor. The poet, in other subjects, walks a broad
road, but here he seems to tread along a line, and the slightest deviation un-
does him"; he falls into vulgarity or insipidity (1:204). This image of the
writer as tightrope walker has its source in Horace, who sees the true dramatic poet, the magician who can first wring the heart and then console it,
as walking a high and perilous wire.[1] Goldsmith's most interesting use of
the image occurs in his discussion of the writer who strikes out for great
beauties, and who therefore takes great risks. "An author who would be
sublime, often runs his thoughts into burlesque; yet I can readily pardon his
mistaking ten times, for once succeeding. True genius walks along a line,
and perhaps our greatest pleasure is in seeing it so often near falling, without being ever actually down" (1:429). The reader, or spectator, is both delighted by the virtuosity and thrilled by the daring and the danger. In art, as
in life, Goldsmith was a gambler, a risk-taker who did not always succeed in
keeping his footing. But the risks have to be run: "The more original . . .
any performance is, the more it is liable to deviate. . . .In literature as in
commerce the value of the acquisition is generally proportioned to the haz-
ard of the adventure" (1:259). Genius, then, is audacity, boldness of imagery and powerful sentiment in the serious genres, adventurousness and
unconventionality in the comic ones.

Hence Goldsmith's disappointment with the odes of Thomas Gray,
whose failing is timorousness, and who is advised by his anonymous reviewer that he should venture "to be more an original" and less an imitator
of the antique. In any case his lofty exercises in the Pindaric manner are addressed to a scholarly elite (thereby incurring the taint of affectation), and
are misjudged, since Gray has not properly considered the temperaments of
his readers. Pindar adjusted his style and language "exactly to the dispositions of his countrymen. Irregular, enthusiastic, and quick in transition, he
wrote for a people inconstant, of warm imaginations, and exquisite sensibility." It is foolishness to address eighteenth-century British readers in this
vein, "a people not easily impressed with new ideas; extremely tenacious of
the old; with difficulty warmed, and as slowly cooling again" (1:112–14).
A sense of national character, sharpened by his travels, is thus part of
Goldsmith's critical system, providing firm, practical guidelines. To succeed
with the British reading public a poet will need to be steadily persuasive,
progressing by means of a carefully managed argument. But once the reader

is won over there will be no necessity for authorial frenzy in order to keep his attention. Even in the theater, where the enthusiasm of some spectators may prove infectious, the dramatist must keep a sharp eye on probability and plausibility, on the persuasive logic of the scene, and must work not by coups de théâtre but by the gradual tightening of tension and the natural evolution of feeling, or what Goldsmith calls "a pleasing gradation of sentiment" (1:12). Arthur Murphy's *Orphan of China* (1759) is faulty because "the pathos begins without a proper preparation of incident" (1:172).

The critic's task is both "to direct our taste" and to "conduct the poet up to perfection" (1:10). The poet, learning from his errors, will grow in excellence and therefore in fame. For fame, in the modest sense of "being remembered with respect" (1:417), is the writer's true goal. "Let none affect to despise future fame . . . this honest ambition of being admired by posterity" (1:307). The adjective "honest," signifying unashamed decency and worthiness, reappears at the end of "The Deserted Village", where poetry is said to "strike for honest fame"; the verb need not imply that poetry is belligerent, merely that it makes its way toward, or aims at, fame.

Goldsmith complains in his "Reverie" (better known as the "Fame Machine" essay) that "Our gentlemen . . . who preside at the distribution of literary fame, seem resolved to part with praise neither from motives of justice or generosity" (1:444). He himself, preoccupied with justice, and by nature warmhearted, is not of their number. As a critic he is happy when concurring with the common reader—Parnell's "The Hermit" is "held in just esteem" (5:319)—and happier still when redressing the balance in favor of a writer unfairly neglected. In *The Beauties of English Poesy* he prints three fables by Edward Moore, "a poet that never had justice done him while living; there are few of the moderns have a more correct taste, or a more pleasing manner of expressing their thoughts" (5:326). His praise is generous and unstinting: an edition of Greek tragedies "is certainly well calculated for the use of schools, and deserves all the encouragement due to the best performances of this kind" (1:131); Nicholas Rowe's lyric, "Despairing beside a clear stream," is "better than anything of the kind in our language" (5:329). Even when praise is introduced by a "perhaps," the effect is to suggest a proper tentativeness, allowing for the possibility of rival contenders without diminishing the warmth of the response: *The Rape of the Lock* is, "perhaps, the most perfect" poem in English (5:319), while Tickell's pseudoballad "Colin and Lucy" is "perhaps the best in our language" (5:327). In the latter case the competition includes of course Goldsmith's own "Edwin and Angelina."

On the other hand, justice also requires that unmerited praise should not go unchecked. The earl of Mulgrave's *Essay upon Poetry* is admitted into Goldsmith's anthology, but carries a prefatory warning that "it has been praised more than it deserves" (5:329). Shenstone's ballads, "chiefly commended for the natural simplicity of the thoughts, and the harmony of the versification" are in fact "not excellent in either" (5:328). In both cases we must reconsider conventional judgments, but not simply in order to set these particular records straight. For as Goldsmith perceived, to praise the undeserving is indirectly to dispraise the meritorious: "Every encouragement given to stupidity, when known to be such, is also a negative insult upon genius." The point is made thus in the *Inquiry* (1:310); it is repeated shortly afterward in the review of Butler's works (1:209).

The topic of praise, its motivation and its effects, appears at the very beginning of Goldsmith's literary career, in his review of John Home's *Douglas: A Tragedy*, and continues to preoccupy him, almost to the point of obsession. Consideration of Home's text is framed by consideration of the text's reception. The review begins by observing, with quietly elegant wit, that circumstances have adventitiously favored the play: "When the town, by a tedious succession of indifferent performances, has been long confined to censure, it will naturally wish for an opportunity of praise, and like a losing gamester, vainly expect every last throw must retrieve the former. In this disposition, a performance with but the slightest share of merit is welcomed with no small share of applause" (1:10). The review ends by noting that the loud praise of one influential individual, David Hume, may have been counterproductive, by exciting envy on the one hand, and raising impossibly high expectations on the other. Moreover, too much adulation is bad for the writer, who acquires a false sense of his own excellence. The fledgling reviewer boldly tells Home that his play is only average. "Let candor allow this writer mediocrity now; his future productions may probably entitle him to higher applause." "Candor" here means both impartiality of judgment and warm or kindly feeling. It is for Home's good that he be told a sour truth.

In his preface to William Guthrie's *General History of the World* (1764), Goldsmith claims that one of the advantages of reading history is that it allows us the luxury of disinterested praise. We can contemplate "the virtues of the good without conscious adulation," that is, without feeling obliged to express our praise, as though it is a blessing to be temporarily free from the burden and tedium of adulation. Works of history also grant us a power that we are normally denied: we can "constitute ourselves judges of the merit of even kings, and thus . . . anticipate what posterity will say of such as now hear only the voice of flattery" (5:278). True assessment is invariably associated in Goldsmith's mind with the dangerous, false assessments of flattery.

At its best, flattery is insipid and futile; George III is not enlightened or informed by the laudatory addresses launched at him by his subjects (3:174–75). It devalues the currency of praise (2:414; 3:175), and demeans both the flatterer and the flattered, since it betrays not admiration but contempt for its subject. At its worst it panders to our vanity, literally turns our heads in frenzied dizziness (3:353), and corrupts us by encouraging affectation, arrogance, megalomania.

Goldsmith never misses an opportunity to scoff at mutual admiration cliques, and the absurd self-satisfaction of those who walk forward to immortality in the warm sunshine of sycophantic applause (1:231, 472, 473–74; 2:15, 309). Obituary and elegy, which are so often the "paltry escutcheons of flattery" (1:166), are also therefore the constant target of his parodic comedy. Letter 106 of *The Citizen of the World* ridicules the conventional pastoral elegy: at Pollio's death "the cows forget to graze, and the very tigers start from the forest with sympathetic concern." The Chinese Philosopher then offers an elegy in a new style, which ingeniously preserves the expected flatteries but saves the day for truth with a bathetic mental reservation at the end of each stanza.

> How sad the groves and plains appear,
> And sympathetic sheep;
> Even pitying hills would drop a tear!
> —*If hills could learn to weep.*

When the elegizing and eulogizing bards are introduced, the true motives of poetical sorrow are revealed:

> His bounty in exalted strain
> Each bard might well display:
> Since none implored relief in vain
> —*That went relieved away.*[2]

In company Goldsmith was forever attempting to counteract the praise of others' talents, most commonly by parading his own. He seems to have had so deep a suspicion that any kind of spoken praise was more than halfway to becoming treacherous flattery, that he wished to stifle adulation at whatever cost to his own image and reputation. His response was so predictable that Johnson wittily remarked, as he was enjoying a brisk coach ride, "This man drives fast and well; were Goldsmith here now he would tell us he could do better."[3] Johnson's commendation would certainly have prompted some such claim, and Goldsmith, who would have regarded Johnson's praise of the driver as virtually a moral provocation, would have been accused (as he invariably was) of having been provoked by envy. The most absurd such accusation concerns his reported remark during a trip to the Continent in the summer of 1770 with the Horneck family. The two Horneck girls were standing on their hotel balcony when some French officers in the square below began complimenting them on their good looks. Goldsmith seemed at first amused, but at length, as Mary Horneck reported, he assumed "something of severity of countenance, which was a peculiarity of his humour often displayed when most disposed to be jocular"; Goldsmith could keep a comically straight face in society as in his writings. Turning aside, he muttered that "Elsewhere he would also have his admirers." Mary was subsequently distressed to find adduced as proof of Goldsmith's envious disposition—as it is by Boswell—what was said in "mere playfulness."[4] The playfulness, however, concealed a reproach. In another version of the anecdote, that of James Northcote, the girls are described as "willing to gratify" their admirers by appearing on the balcony.[5] If they were succumbing to flattery, if their vanity was being nourished, then it was time for their companion to create a diversion and to issue a warning against the insincerity and moral danger of such attentions. The best gloss on Goldsmith's muttered remark is supplied by his discussion in chapter 2 of the *Inquiry* of that "agreeable trifling which . . . often deceives us into instruction. . . . The finest sentiment, and the most weighty truth, may put on a pleasing face, and it is even virtuous to jest when serious advice might be disgusting" (1:319).

It is not quite out of the question that in seeming to praise himself Goldsmith was sometimes uttering praise of another, though in a manner so oblique as to be almost invisible. To claim to be as good a raconteur as Garrick, and then to produce a yarn in the rambling manner of Beau Nash, is to leave Garrick's reputation unscathed, perhaps even enhanced. There *is* an art of the anecdote, though Goldsmith has signally failed to master it. Similarly, to decry Burke's oratorical skill, when a group of friends is warm in its praise, by declaring that "speechifying is all a knack," but failing, when called on to speak, to produce more than a sentence, looks like a calculated way of declaring the contrary.[6] The stuffy atmosphere of laudation is cleared away by Goldsmith's foolery and apparent discomfiture; at the same time he has comically demonstrated that Burke really is exceptional. It was Johnson's opinion that "There is no sport in mere praise when people are all of a mind."⁷ It was Goldsmith's role to introduce an element of sport.

Goldsmith, after all, believed that "Counsels . . . as well as compliments, are best conveyed in an indirect and oblique manner" (5:227), and shared with Swift, from whom he probably learnt the technique, a fondness for raillery, for commending someone by appearing to discommend—a mode of irony that reverses the more common technique of blame-by-apparent-praise. Fulsomeness is thus avoided, and the surprising verbal turn flatters the intelligence of the recipient. Goldsmith practices raillery early and late. In a letter from Edinburgh to Robert Bryanton he assumes a rough indifference to the charms of Bryanton's sisters; he is not, he says, affected by their fine skins, fine eyes, or good sense.⁸ At the close of "The Haunch of Venison," a verse epistle probably written in 1770 and addressed to Viscount Clare, fellow Irishman, fellow poet, and fellow joker, Goldsmith pretends to be downright rude: "To be plain, my good lord, it's but labor misplaced, To send such good verses to one of your taste." For there must be something imperfect in the taste of one who modestly thinks "so very slightly" of his own poetry.

Raillery works best among friends. In mixed companies, or when retailed at secondhand, this kind of masked sincerity or innocent indirectness can be badly misconstrued. Goldsmith confessed that he risked being misinterpreted precisely because he was afraid of being so, afraid that his worthy motives would be suspected of being base and mercenary. The crucial document is a letter to his cousin, Jane Lawder, the married daughter of Thomas Contarine, in which he explains why he had discontinued writing to his uncle while abroad: "I could not continue a correspondence where *every* acknowlegement for past favours might be considered as an indirect request for future ones." Similar reasoning has produced similar unconventionalities: "I have often affected bluntness to avoid the imputation of flattery, have frequently seem'd to overlook those merits too obvious to escape notice, and pretended disregard to those instances of good nature and good sense which I could not fail tacitly to applaud; and all this lest I should be rank'd among the grinning tribe who say very true to all that is said . . . and who had rather be reckoning the money in your pocket than the virtue in your breast."⁹ Goldsmith's attachment to justice arises from a deep fear of being misjudged.

This letter was written in August 1758. The same scrupulous anxieties about the purity of his motives had already been voiced in the first paragraph of his first preface, to his translation of Marteilhe's *Mémoires d'un Protestant,* published six months earlier: "The praise by which a translator attempts to advance the reputation of his original, is usually considered as an indirect claim to applause on his own account." The "usually" is striking in its exaggeration. Who would have reached this cynical conclusion if Goldsmith himself had not pointed the way? Though the translator, he goes on to say, "may not stand in the full luster of his own panegyric, yet such are his connections with his author that he receives it by reflection, and tacitly compliments himself, at least for judgment in his choice" (5:222–23). It is hard that so subtle an analyst of the self-regarding instincts, one so alert to vanity and the most elusive manifestations of self-congratulation, should have been so universally condemned for these very faults.

It is with the critic as with the translator. "The praise which is every day lavished upon Virgil, Horace, or Ovid, is often no more than an indirect method the critic takes to compliment his own discernment" (1:152). So begins Goldsmith's review of Barrett's translation of Ovid's *Epistles.* The same argument, similarly phrased, presents itself in the chapter "Upon Criticism" in the *Inquiry* (1:322), and resurfaces in an essay contributed to the *Weekly Magazine* in January 1760 (3:52–53). It is more fully developed— the frequency of repetition is exceptional even by Goldsmith's standards —in a hostile review, also published in 1760, of Roger Kedington's *Critical Dissertations upon the Iliad of Homer.* Kedington is the Homeric apologist par excellence: "Pope, one would have thought, had bepraised the Grecian sufficiently, saw more in Homer than Homer knew, and vigorously defended him almost through thick and thin; but this writer regards Pope as a faithless asserter of his master's cause, as having given up several posts that were tenable, and even of sometimes siding with the enemy" (1:218). Kedington goes well beyond common sense in his enthusiasm for the divine, the incomparable, the faultless Homer. Unfortunately for him, his reviewer knows only too well what lies behind this rapturous nonsense: "The praise bestowed on a writer of established reputation, is perhaps more frequently designed as a compliment to ourselves than the author. We only show the rectitude of our own taste by a standard allowed already to be just. What advantages the public are to gain by praising Homer at this time of day, we know not. Mr. Kedington may reap some, since all must allow he has taste enough to relish those beauties which most men of taste have either relished, or pretended to relish, before" (1:213–14). It is an argument that must give pause to all critics, including critics of Goldsmith.

Extending Horizons

Goldsmith's first major work, the *Inquiry into the Present State of Polite Learning in Europe* (1759), tackles the question of judgment on a broad front. As its final chapter dryly admits, it is in the nature of any intellectual endeavor that it should produce a distorted view of things: "Every subject acquires an adventitious importance to him who considers it with application. He finds it more closely connected with human happiness than the rest of mankind are apt to allow" (1:336). We recognize here the "personal estimate" that Matthew Arnold was to consider one of the major obstacles to objective judgment. This is not the only anticipation of Arnold's position. His eagerness to counter the blinkered provinciality of Victorian England through the advocacy of European values is similar to Goldsmith's advocacy of a social and cultural ideal summed up in the phrase "a citizen of the world." Though he did not originate the phrase, Goldsmith made it very much his own, most famously as the title of his collected "Chinese Letters." But its first appearance in his work is in the *Inquiry,* where it is applied to "the learned who look beyond the bounds of national prejudice" (1:291).

So Goldsmith invites us to acknowledge the best that is being done abroad. He draws attention to the individual achievements of the Danish Baron Holberg, of the Swedish Count Tessin, of Maffei and Metastasio, and to the corporate achievements of the Berlin Academy. The aim is to broaden insular horizons, to promote different and superior ways of doing things. The matter of patronage, for example, is better ordered in France: "The French nobility have certainly a most pleasing way of satisfying the vanity of an author, without indulging his avarice. A man of literary merit is sure of being caressed by the great, though seldom enriched. His pension from the crown just supplies half a competence, and the sale of his labors makes some small addition to his circumstances; thus the author leads a life of splendid poverty, and seldom becomes wealthy or indolent enough to discontinue an exertion of those abilities by which he rose." The contrast with England, in this respect a land of extremes, is evident and instructive: "our writers of rising merit are generally neglected, while the few of an established reputation are overpaid by a luxurious affluence" (1:298–99). The English patrons, the men of power and influence, should not, however, be blamed overmuch. Their attitude to authors is only the particular operation of a national characteristic. As everyone knows, the English are reserved, slow to make friends, "but violent in friendships once contracted." Among such a people literary merit can only struggle painfully toward recognition, but once recognized will be "violently" rewarded, feted, and lionized. An understanding of national character not only explains the shortcomings of the English way of patronage, but also excuses it. How can wealthy Englishmen, being English, behave otherwise?

As an expatriate observer and amateur anthropologist, Goldsmith is fascinated by the differences between the nations and races of the world, by the variety that a prospect of society reveals. Before the *Inquiry*, he had set ancient Greeks against eighteenth-century Englishmen in his review of Gray's *Odes*. Shortly after it, in a series of four essays contributed to the *Royal Magazine* (June–September 1760; 3:66–86) he surveys mankind, as a "returning wanderer," from Lapland to the South Seas. The more he explores these interesting differences, the more powerfully formative he finds them. The nature and quality of a whole country's literary output can be directly referred to its people's predominant qualities; it has been bred in their bones. So a French writer has, as part of his birthright, a large measure of self-confidence. The air he breathes exudes satisfaction with all things French. No marvel then that the uninhibited and self-assured Frenchman, "by not being dazzled at the splendor of another's reputation," may mark out for himself an unbeaten path to fame (1:298). The French are not cowed by the glories of their predecessors. There has not therefore been the same falling-off from the achievements of seventeenth-century French authors, as there has been from the Elizabethan era in England.

National character being so inescapably powerful a molding force, it follows, despite the opposing pull of Goldsmith's cosmopolitanism, that "every country should have a national system of criticism" (1:296). One must accept that what pleases French temperaments cannot always please English ones. Since the English are by nature more realistic and grave than the French, less cheerful about the present and more inclined to suicide, it is inevitable that death will be treated very differently in the drama of the two countries. The English find "nothing hideous" in a corpse-strewn stage, because they "look upon death as an incident no way terrible, but sometimes fly to it for refuge from the calamities of life." The French will of course be disgusted by such visible slaughter. They may flatter themselves that in keeping death offstage they are obeying classical precedent, but that argument is mere rationalization. They do not wish to look on death because they are cheerfully content with life, and because they are rather escapist. The thrust of the logic is liberating—readers and spectators are freed from false, because inappropriate, critical criteria such as the neoclassical rules—but at the same time pessimistic. If the English are cautious in friendship, constitutionally slow to reward merit, there is little hope that their treatment of authors will improve. They can note and admire what is done in France, but they will go on as before. The centripetal tendency of national peculiarities negates and finally overcomes the centrifugal movement toward citizenship of the world.

As there are contradictory impulses in the argument of the *Inquiry* so there are uncomfortable extremes in its style. On the one hand is a cautious timidity—"if I may so express it"; "it may be allowed that"—together with frequent occurrences of "possibly," "probably," "perhaps." A "concessive attitude," as Robert Hopkins has noted, is a distinctive feature of Goldsmith's prose style, and contributes to the often-remarked amiability of his work.[10] In the *Inquiry,* however, this trait comes across rather as an unnecessary tentativeness, an almost excessive deferentiality, since it coexists with some remarkably sweeping generalizations and bold assertions—"The Marquis d'Argens attempts to add the character of a philosopher to the vices of a debauchee"; "Our stage is more magnificent than any other in Europe"—and with some stridently aggressive images:

But it would be endless to recount all the insect-like absurdities which were hatched in the schools of those specious idlers [that is, the critics and commentators of the late Roman Empire]. Be it sufficient to say, that they increased as learning improved, but swarmed on its decline . . . . Metrodorus, Valerius Probus, Aulus Gellius, Pedianus, Boethius, and an hundred others, to be acquainted with whom might show much reading, and but little judgment—these, I say, made choice each of an author, and delivered all their load of learning on his back. Shame to our ancestors! Many of their [the commentators'] works have reached our times entire, while Tacitus himself has suffered mutilation. (1:267)

When Goldsmith revised the *Inquiry* for a second edition, shortly before his death, the word "insect-like" was dropped. The phrase "the vile complexion of the times," used twice in the first edition (1:307, 328), appears only once in the second. Such revisions suggest that Goldsmith recognized his earlier intemperate language as that of an angry young man, impatient with all that obstructed the path of the youthful aspirant to fame.

Though Goldsmith's declared aim is to attempt to remedy the "approaching decay" of taste and learning (1:258), the tenor of the writing is often that of a man still smarting from the experience of hackwork, depressed by the "solemnity of manner" prevailing in poetry, pessimistic about the future of drama, which is in the hands of avaricious and power-hungry theater managers, and particularly gloomy because the prevailing taste has, "in effect, banished new comedies from the stage" (1:321). The recurrent imagery of crowds, of competition for fame, of smothering and suffocating, reinforces the gloom, as does the imagery of loads and weights—the pressure of convention, vested interests, and apathy that is too heavy for any single individual to lift. When Goldsmith wrote the essay he still had hopes of a medical career in India, of turning his back on Europe. The essay is in some sense a farewell to European culture, a farewell occasionally serene and appreciative, but not infrequently bitter.

One of Goldsmith's strengths as a writer is the versatility that Johnson handsomely recognized, both in his epitaph—"Poet, Naturalist, Historian; who touched almost every kind of writing . . ."—and in his private conversation: "Whether, indeed, we take him as a poet,—as a comick writer,—or as an historian, he stands in the first class."[11] The corresponding weakness is miscellaneousness, and the lure of the miscellaneous was something that Goldsmith found difficult to resist. (The *Inquiry* suffers from a certain randomness, most obviously in the chapter on university education, confessedly an assemblage of unconnected thoughts.) It must have seemed to Goldsmith that he could happily indulge this impulse in the medium of the periodical essay, both by turning out essays on interestingly varied topics for other men's magazines—and from the autumn of 1759 to the summer of 1762 his contributions were many and varied—and even more satisfyingly, by producing an entire periodical himself. The publisher John Wilkie gave him his opportunity, and in early October 1759 Wilkie's press advertisement promised a new weekly: "THE BEE. Consisting of Variety of Essays, on the Amusements, Follies, and Vices in Fashion." This was not the first literary bee (Eustace Budgell had edited one in the 1730s), but originality of title was probably less important than aptness. In his opening editorial Goldsmith promises that, like the industrious insect whose name he is using, he will rove from flower to flower, "with seeming inattention, but concealed choice" (1:354n). There are more types of blossom than the advertisement promised, not only essays on social life, morality, and literature, but also an article on natural history (a sly joke, since it is mainly about spiders), biographical sketches, poems, and stories. Each number contains six or more items; some, like the long essay on education, are serious affairs, while others exemplify that "agreeable trifling" whose scarcity Goldsmith had lamented in the *Inquiry*.

Much of the serious material is secondhand, a phenomenon not unexpected by its first readers. As Robert Mayo has said, miscellanies "were, by long sufferance, a predatory species of publication"; they were in their very nature, as the editor of one of them claimed, "repositories for meritorious papers" already in print elsewhere, and therefore stood exempt from the charge of plagiarism.[12] More positively, Goldsmith could take credit for opening up to English readers, in his unpretentious pages, important aspects of contemporary French thought. Robert Hopkins has rightly emphasized Goldsmith's role as cultural middleman, disseminating "the refined elegance of the French Enlightenment."[13] The seminal *Encyclopédie* provides the first half of Goldsmith's study of eloquence, and an even greater proportion of his essay on political frugality. More significantly, because more than refined elegance is in question, from its pages come warnings against all that makes for discord: war, faction, envy, superstition, bigotry, prejudice. Its account of Hypasia is a harsh indictment of religious rancor. To similar effect two letters of Voltaire are translated: the first ironically contemplates the horrors of the Seven Years War, "these great events of the best of possible systems" (1:369); the second unequivocally commends toleration, tranquillity, and the cultivation of learning "without divisions or envy" (1:392). In the same vein Goldsmith reprints material about witchhunts from an English periodical of 1720.

Social harmony may be promoted by combating the forces of destruction and ridiculing narrow-mindedness. It may also be fostered (though Goldsmith, as we have seen, has reservations about the possibility of modifying national character) by letting the English observe their antisocial gloom and reserve through another's eyes, those, for example, of the Abbé Le Blanc. So he reprints one of Le Blanc's *Letters on the English and French Nations,* offering his readers an image of French sociability and gaiety. What is delightful about the French is their capacity for being delighted, their readiness to express "laughter inspired by joy" (1:492). This chimes with Goldsmith's personal demand for liveliness and comic vitality in literature, particularly in that most social form of literature, the drama (1:359–63, 450–52).

Goldsmith's bee is certainly no drone, though he is fearful lest his writing be censured as dronish and dull. His wish to achieve variety, to create "a studied difference in subject and style" between one item and the next (1:357), results in some startling juxtapositions. The penultimate item in the fourth number is the much anthologized "A City Night-Piece," which meditates on the "emptiness of human vanity," and envisages the now deserted city as a scene of future desolation, before turning to the suffering and distress of the houseless poor. The next and final item touches on poverty and beggary too, but in a very different vein: this is the mock-elegy on Mrs. Mary Blaize, pawnbroker:

The needy seldom passed her door,
And always found her kind;
She freely lent to all the poor—
Who left a pledge behind.

To follow an atmospheric prose poem with a jokey squib is to push the
principle of variety beyond its limits, to descend into heterogeneity. In spite
of Goldsmith's promise that his bee's rovings would not be random, that a
"concealed choice" would operate, there is little sense of editorial principles
at work, because there is little sense of a steady editorial personality. In the
"Remarks on our Theatres" a kindly pontificator is very lightly sketched in:
"As I love to be advising too, for advice is easily given, and bears a show of
wisdom and superiority" (1:359). A slightly cynical, slightly weary individual is fleetingly glimpsed elsewhere—"Every man who has seen the world"
(1:395)—while the pleasantly comic piece "On Dress" purports to be
narrated by one who will be "sixty-two the twelfth of next November"
(1:375n). These hints remain unconnected and undeveloped. Where we
might have expected an editorial presence to emerge, in the opening statement of intent, we find something else. Instead of projecting a persona in
the manner of Mr. Spectator, or the Idler, or even Fitzadam of the *World*,
Goldsmith gives us, disarmingly, an image of the Anxious Author, his
"power of pleasing . . . damped by solicitude, and his cheerfulness dashed
with apprehension" (1:353n). What follows is a brilliant representation of
what we might call page-fright: "whichever way I turned, nothing presented
but prospects of terror, despair, chandlers' shops, and waste paper." In such
a state of nerves, it is only to be expected that attitude and tone will be unstable. The writer is now self-deprecatory, now shrugging off anticipated
complaints, and now scorning the showier efforts of his competitors. He is
by turns diffident, cordial, nonchalant, overemphatic, cocky. We witness
"natural humor" turning to "pertness," and factitious "vivacity" taking the
place of "real wit."
    As a carefully calculated dramatization of a beginning author's plight,
this is well-nigh perfect. It may have struck readers, however, as somewhat
unseemly, too much of a personal confession, which is indeed how Goldsmith refers to his next editorial intervention, at the beginning of the fourth
number. He is still as frank as when he first set out, equally droll, but more
despondent when he considers the sales of rival magazines: "while the works
of others fly like unpinioned swans, I find my own move as heavily as a
new-plucked goose" (1:415). The public was perhaps unprepared for such
candor. The personal note, the bared bosom, might have been a factor in the

poor sales. In any case the strain of producing single-handed a 32-page weekly journal soon began to tell. In the seventh and eighth numbers Goldsmith does what he was later to censure other magazines for doing to him: he reprints recent material—three essays from the *Literary Magazine* of the previous year—without acknowledgment. Even where he provides his own introductory and concluding paragraphs, as with "An Account of the Augustan Age of England," he is not being strictly original, for he there recycles ideas from the *Inquiry* and from earlier numbers of the *Bee* itself. In reading Goldsmith one often has a strong sense of déjà vu. He quarries vigorously from others, but equally vigorously from himself.

Even with the aid of translated and borrowed material, Goldsmith could not keep his bee aloft. It came to an abrupt end just two months and eight numbers after it had launched itself into flight, on 24 November 1759. Coincidentally, the beginning of Goldsmith's first masterpiece was only another two months away: the series of "Chinese Letters," better known as *The Citizen of the World*. Here, adopting the guise of a Chinese philosopher, Goldsmith could safely revel in variety. His Chinese gentleman observes diverse aspects of British life and British folly, and utters his observations with a distinct, and distinctive, voice. The author of the *Bee* had felt uncomfortable about assuming "an air of impudence." The author of the "Chinese Letters" could assume a mask and feel completely at ease.

Chapter Three
The Observant Exile

The Citizen of the World

On Thursday, 24 January 1760, among the news columns of the *Public Ledger,* a recently inaugurated London daily, its readers encountered two letters. The first, addressed from Amsterdam to a merchant in London, briefly introduces and recommends its bearer, a native of Honan in China. The second is from Lien Chi Altangi, the Chinese mandarin himself. He thanks his host in Amsterdam, describes the terrors of the sea crossing (his first) to England, and gives his impressions of the capital. From this unobtrusive beginning grew Goldsmith's most substantial literary work. The "Chinese Letters" continued to appear, usually twice weekly, throughout 1760, and thereafter with diminishing frequency until 14 August 1761, by which date they totaled 119. Thoroughly revised, rearranged, and expanded, they were published in book form on 1 May 1762. The 123 letters had now become *The Citizen of the World.*

The beginnings of the enterprise, like those of the *Bee,* are modest. Unlike the *Bee*'s they are confident. Several notes are firmly struck in the second letter: the pseudo-oriental manner—"Friend of my heart, may the wings of peace rest upon thy dwelling"; Altangi's naive bluntness—"You have been bred a merchant, and I a scholar; you consequently love money better than I," an audacious stroke, since the *Public Ledger* was primarily a businessman's journal; Altangi's status as a "poor philosophic wanderer"; his bewilderments and misconceptions as a stranger in London, exemplified by his comic inability to (literally) read the signs:

The houses borrow very few ornaments from architecture; their chief decoration seems to be a paltry piece of painting, hung out at their doors or windows, at once a proof of their indigence and vanity. Their vanity in each having one of those pictures exposed to public view, and their indigence in being unable to get them better painted. In this respect, the fancy of their painters is also deplorable. Could you believe it? I have seen five black lions and three blue boars in less than a circuit of half a mile, and yet you know that animals of these colours are nowhere to be found except in the wild imaginations of Europe.[1]

The joke, darting in several directions at once, is typical of Goldsmith. We smile at the observer, baffled by alien conventions; at the oddity of inn signs that we normally take for granted (there is, after all, something wildly imaginative about a blue boar), and at the paucity of invention of those who name inns and paint their signs: *five* black lions.

However distinctive the touch, there was nothing new in the conception. When he was a student in Edinburgh Goldsmith jocularly remarked that he was "as recluse as the Turkish Spy at Parris,"[2] alluding to G. P. Marana's *Letters of a Turkish Spy* (English translation, 1687). More recent, and much more searching, were Montesquieu's *Lettres persanes* (1721), imitated by George Lyttelton in his *Letters from a Persian in England to His Friend at Ispahan* (1735), while the Marquis d'Argens, with his *Lettres chinoises* (1739), had further exploited the satirical and subversive possibilities of a foreign eye turned on European attitudes and institutions.

To the work of these predecessors Goldsmith liberally helped himself. His topics are frequently theirs: vanity and flattery, luxury and colonialism, learning and justice. Indeed, whole paragraphs are theirs too, while the list of other creditors is extensive: Marivaux, Buffon, travel writers, and English periodical essayists, including Johnson. Nor, as usual, does Goldsmith omit to draw upon himself. We must concede that his mind was not, to take the obvious but tough comparison, as fertile as Johnson's, and that when time and inspiration were short he simply followed the line of least resistance.[3] We may mitigate his plagiarisms by the plea that, as in his earlier publications, he was aiming to make available in England some of the interesting and provocative material that was being produced abroad. Altangi is a true "cosmopolite" (2:426) by virtue of his creator's literary borrowings.

There are differences of emphasis and structure between Goldsmith and his most immediate models. Lyttelton is more political. Montesquieu and d'Argens have more extensive preoccupations and a larger cast of letter writers. Not that Goldsmith is narrow in range. The majority of Altangi's letters are addressed to his friend and mentor Fum Hoam in Peking; from Peking he receives in turn five epistles. He is also in correspondence with his son Hingpo, who like Telemachus follows his father's steps across the Asian wilderness, and who undergoes romantic adventures. Hingpo becomes the captive of a Persian tyrant, and is captivated by a European slave girl destined for the tyrant's bed. They escape together, are separated, make their independent ways to London, and are united in marriage. It had taken Altangi 700 "painful days" to reach England; his son requires some 18 months, and the intermittent charting of his progress through Tartary, Persia, Circassia, and Russia makes us keenly aware of the dimensions of space and time. Goldsmith's emphasis falls repeatedly on the "remote regions," the "many thousand miles," the "immeasurable distance" or "immeasurable wilds" that separate Altangi from his native land. Goldsmith apparently first toyed with the idea of using a visitor from North Africa, or yet another Persian, as his expatriate commentator.[4] But through the figure of a Chinese he could more naturally give fuller expression to what haunted his imagination, and perhaps his conscience: his own remoteness and alienation, the pain of exile. The greater the distance, the greater the distress, as Altangi tells Hoam in his first letter: "those ties that bind me to my native country, and you, are still unbroken. By every remove I only drag a greater length of chain" (2:21). The same ambivalent image appears four years later in "The Traveller," when the poet measures the physical and psychological space between his wandering self and his brother Henry, enjoying a settled domestic bliss in Ireland:

> Where'er I roam, whatever realms to see,
> My heart, untravelled, fondly turns to thee,
> Still to my brother turns, with ceaseless pain,
> And drags at each remove a lengthening chain.
> (ll.7–10; 4:249)

A chain may represent an emotional bond of patriotism, loyalty, filial or fraternal affection. A chain that is dragged suggests more starkly a prisoner, a slave held against his will, tethered to a country, a locale, a family from which he cannot break free to claim his independence. Both the poet and Altangi would be rid of their chains if they could.

Though to all appearances a voluntary exile from Ireland, Goldsmith probably felt that he had been banished by a disapproving family, and specifically rejected by a hostile mother. Altangi is certainly an official exile. He has left China without the permission of the emperor, the authority figure who lurks in the background. He has set out on a journey of curiosity, sightseeing on a global scale, and he is accordingly punished: his family and goods are seized. (His family are therefore the real sufferers. Was Goldsmith taking a vicarious revenge?) Goldsmith knew from experience that the restless individual can be punished and can punish himself. Altangi may see himself as a "philosophic wanderer," while Hingpo politely calls his father a "travelling philosopher." Fum Hoam, however, addresses his friend on four occasions as a "discontented wanderer," and in the debate on traveling and restless curiosity that runs as a minor thread through *The Citizen of the World,* Hoam is the voice of stay-at-home reason. An "enthusiasm for knowledge," he argues, simply obstructs happiness, tears the traveler from "all the connections that make life pleasing," and sentences him to a life of solitary anxiety (2:37). Hoam's censure of Altangi for following intellectual will-o'-the-wisps (2:176) reinforces the admonitory allegory communicated by Hingpo (Letter 37), of the audacious youth who climbs, Rasselas-like, out of the contented valley and (unlike Rasselas) meets destruction: "they who travel in pursuit of wisdom walk only in a circle [as though tethered], and, after all their labor, at last return to their pristine ignorance." Similarly, Hoam's argument that happiness depends upon combining mental with emotional and sensuous satisfactions, and that Altangi is denying himself the latter, is supported by Altangi's own narrative of the restless Prince Bonbenin, who forsakes the "innocent pleasures of matrimony" (2:206) in pursuit of the illusory white mouse with green eyes. Finally, the autobiography of the "philosophic cobbler" who has lived an unsettled life (Letter 65), offers a comically diminished image of Altangi's wanderings, while also revealing that for some natures, like Goldsmith's, traveling and gambling are two sides of the same coin: "some unforeseen misfortune, or a desire of trying my luck elsewhere, has removed me perhaps a whole mile away from my former customers."

The citizen of the world, intellectually at home everywhere, is emotionally at home nowhere. He is the type of the lonely wanderer, more fleetingly represented by Catherine Alexowna, the poor solitary who becomes empress of Russia (Letter 62), the "wandering beggar" of Letter 92, the "strangers, wanderers, and orphans" of Letter 117 (the "City Night-Piece," borrowed from the *Bee*), and the nomads of Central Asia (2:47, 95, 337). Wandering is a primitive condition, and the lot of the poor. A civilized and well-to-do man who commits himself to such an existence must seem perverse, particularly if his goal is the ever-receding mirage called happiness. The Man in Black, Altangi's English friend and companion, is in the same plight. He has been involved for ten years in a lawsuit. He has, he says, "travelled forward with victory ever in my view, but ever out of reach" (2:390). Once again the parallel with "The Traveller" is compelling. Having painted an idealized picture of his brother's contentment, the poet laments:

> But me, not destined such delights to share,
> My prime of life in wandering spent, and care,
> Impelled, with steps unceasing, to pursue
> Some fleeting good, that mocks me with the view,
> That, like the circle bounding earth and skies,
> Allures from far, yet as I follow flies;

My fortune leads to traverse realms alone,
And find no spot of all the world my own.
(ll.23–30; 4:249–50)

There is also, as Arthur Friedman points out in a note to these lines, a more gloomy parallel with *The Vicar of Wakefield,* where in his prison sermon the Vicar pictures death mocking "the weary traveler with the view," and like the horizon, still flying before him (4:163). The traditional journey through life is, in Goldsmith's despondent moods, a journey along bad roads and with poor accommodation (2:381), undertaken by travelers without maps: "Mankind wanders, unknowing his way, from morning till the evening. Where shall we turn after happiness? Or is it wisest to desist from the pursuit?" (2:96).

Baffled travelers, however, are not solely objects of pity. The comic action of *She Stoops to Conquer* begins when two young men have lost their way, and concludes, after the disorientation of two female coach passengers, with those young men arriving at their goals. Traveling can end in achievement, for it should in theory broaden the mind, purge our insularity, and fortify us "against the accidents of fortune, or the accesses of despair" (2:41)—so Altangi justifies himself to Hoam. The real traveler, he claims, "leaves home to mend himself and others," for in reporting on his journeyings he will foster a real cosmopolitanism, and help to "unite the world." He can at the very least open our eyes to the technology of other nations: the vegetable dyes of India, or a method of distilling spirits from milk practiced by the Siberian Tartars (Letter 108). This letter might be read as a puff for a scheme that Goldsmith had proposed 18 months earlier, and that he continued to entertain: a subsidized expedition to the East for purposes of scientific discovery. Johnson sneered that in his ignorant enthusiasm Goldsmith "would bring home a grinding-barrow, which you see in every street in London, and think that he had furnished a wonderful improvement."[5] Nevertheless, Goldsmith played his part in popularizing science, contributing short articles to the *Public Ledger* on medical and agricultural developments abroad (3:160–67). One of his last projects was a "Dictionary of Arts and Sciences," to be edited by himself; one of his last compilations was the eight-volume *History of the Earth and Animated Nature.*

Furthermore, movement is necessary to man; without it he would stagnate. "Every alteration of place will diversify the prospect" (2:468)— "prospect" being both what is looked at, and what is looked forward to—for even the most beautiful of prospects will pall if it is unchanging. At the end of the book, therefore, Altangi prepares not to settle down in the neighborhood of his son and daughter-in-law, whose journeyings have agreeably ended in a lovers' meeting, but to continue his travels. Confucius, appropriately, has the last, paradoxical word: "They must often change . . . who would be constant in happiness or wisdom."

Not being a penurious wanderer, Altangi can indulge to the full his inquisitive appetite. The poor cobbler brusquely tells him: "Your bread is baked; you may go and see sights the whole day" (2:269). Some sights, such as the tombs of the English monarchs in Westminster Abbey, were on every eighteenth-century tourist's route. These memorials to the dead have indeed been reduced to a show, presided over by an uncouth, mercenary guide (Letter 13). Lower down the social scale, the lying-in-state of a deceased tradesman creates a "disagreeable spectacle" to which flock "all the idlers in town" (2:55). Social life, as the foreigner observes it, is a sequence of puzzling shows and ceremonials. At the bedecking of the modern fine gentleman it is the barber who presides as master of ceremonies (Letter 3). In the theater that function belongs to the noisy, self-willed spectators in the upper galleries, while the dramatic entertainment is furnished not only by the actors but also by the audience: the wits are present to display their taste, while in the boxes ladies and gentlemen play their own little comedies of intrigue (Letter 21).

Altangi claims to receive less satisfaction from seeing a "pageant" than from observing those who observe it. The spectators reveal their pleasure or their envy, and betray their secret wishes to the man who watches them (2:268). He is also aware that others enjoy observing him. The oddity of his looks makes him a wonder to be gazed at, even a sport of nature to the narrow-minded Londoners. They ridicule him in the public walks, where he and Beau Tibbs are "laughed at . . . by every spectator" (2:229), or treat him with private condescension as an object for their entertainment. Invited to an English home for dinner, Altangi finds that he is there purely to satisfy the guests' curiosity, though they prove to be already well informed about oriental habits: "when chairs were drawn for the rest of the company, I was assigned my place on a cushion on the floor" (2:143). The English are inordinately fond of shows and monsters (Letter 45), and Altangi's creator knows what it is to be treated as an oddity. In his preface to the collected *Citizen of the World* Goldsmith compares himself to "one of those solitary animals that has been forced from its forest to gratify human curiosity. My earliest wish was to escape unheeded through life, but I have been set up for half-pence, to fret and scamper at the end of my chain" (2:15). This chain is quite unambivalent.

To observe without being observed oneself is an exclusively oriental way of proceeding, something that Altangi has left behind. The Chinese lady spies on her lover through a screen (2:168), and the Japanese emperor and his ladies view from behind lattices the spectacle of the groveling European merchants (2:456). But Western society makes being seen as important as, if not more important than, seeing, for on being seen depends one's sense of being, one's identity. At the level of comedy we have the foppish colonel of Letter 39, whose besotted admirer "first saw him at Ranelagh. He shines there; he's nothing without Ranelagh, and Ranelagh nothing without him." "Nothing without Ranelagh" is exact. Deprived of the context of the fashionable assembly, the place in which he is seen, this shadow of a man would simply disappear. Vauxhall Gardens, a rather more popular place of entertainment than Ranelagh, is also important for establishing identities, for there Londoners "show their best clothes, and best faces" (2:293). Letter 71 describes an evening spent at Vauxhall by a rather assorted group: Altangi and the Man in Black, a pawnbroker's widow much admired by the latter, and Mr. and Mrs. Tibbs. On their arrival Altangi notes that the well-dressed throngs are "looking satisfaction"; the phrase intimates that they are pleased with what they see, and pleased with themselves. After some nicely observed altercation between the ladies of the party—pseudogentility versus material prosperity—there arises the problem of seating arrangements for their proposed meal: "Mr. and Mrs. Tibbs would sit in none but a genteel box, a box where they might see and be seen, one, as they expressed it, in the very focus of public view. But such a box was not easy to be obtained, for though we were perfectly convinced of our own gentility, and the gentility of our appearance, yet we found it a difficult matter to persuade the keepers of the boxes to be of our opinion." If only others would see us as we see ourselves.

Our dependence on those who regard us is more sardonically treated in an earlier letter, number 67, which depicts the life of a man guided by books rather than by experience, and by his imprudent behavior reduced to poverty. Unfortunately, the treatises he has read "have described poverty in most charming colors, and even his vanity is touched in thinking that he shall show the world, in himself, one more example of patience, fortitude, and resignation." The world will witness his virtues; he will be seen to be exemplary. But poverty comes in a more unpleasing form than he had imagined. Goldsmith sustains the visual motif by slipping into personification, and supposing the philosopher visited by a pageant of abstractions. "Foremost in the hideous procession" is "Contempt with pointing finger." Contempt is at least singling him out, giving him an identity, however contemptible. Worse is to come: "The poor man now finds that

he can get no kings to look at him while he is eating. He finds that in proportion as he grows poor, the world turns its back upon him, and gives
him leave to act the philosopher in all the majesty of solitude. It might be
agreeable enough to play the philosopher while we are conscious that
mankind are spectators, but what signifies wearing the mask of sturdy
contentment, and mounting the stage of restraint, when not one creature
will assist at the exhibition" (2:278). The theatrical context of that last
sentence leads us to take "assist at" as a gallicism, signifying "be present
at," or "witness"; but we cannot altogether overlook the sense of "help
with." We need spectators to assist us to create our own meaningfulness.
The human comedy requires an audience of fellow players.

This poor man is in precisely the opposite situation to that of "the great,"
who are always in the public eye, always on stage, and never lacking an audience. Yet however they may flatter themselves as to their own importance,
they act out their parts purely for the benefit of that audience. "For our
pleasure, and not their own, they sweat under a cumbrous heap of finery.
For our pleasure . . . the slow parading pageant, with all the gravity of grandeur, moves in review" (2:267). Paradoxically, the great become more fortunate in distress, for then we are called upon, by the press and popular report,
to be spectators of tragedy, and "to gaze at the noble sufferers; they have at
once the comfort of admiration and pity" (2:458), and their calamities are
made more bearable. As Altangi asks: "Where is the magnanimity of bearing misfortunes when the whole world is looking on? Men in such circumstances can act bravely even from motives of vanity. . . . The miseries of the
poor are, however, entirely disregarded." It is to make us regard such miseries that the narrative of the disabled veteran is then unfolded.

One effect of so much emphasis on observation and spectacle is to keep
the reader at a critical distance from what Altangi describes. Just as Goldsmith the reviewer had held out "specimens" to his periodical readers, invit-
ing them to pass judgment on these samples of writing, so Altangi offers
carefully culled or carefully invented "specimens": the mock-panegyric
verses on an actress (Letter 85), and the mock-elegiac verses on Pollio; an account of a journey to Kentish Town (Letter 122), done "in the manner of
modern voyagers," complete with faulty speculations, spurious etymologiz-
ing, and topographical trivia. A specimen newspaper hits off national weaknesses (Letter 5), while Goldsmith delights, like Swift, in reproducing in
concentrated form the clichés of pretentious connoisseurs (Letter 34), and of
polite conversation ("he has infinite taste, that's flat!" [Letter 39]), the jar-
gon of the racetrack (Letter 86), and of the smooth-talking shopkeeper
(Letter 77), and the language of fashionable Eastern Tales: "his hair, which

hung like the willow weeping over the glassy stream, was so beautiful that it seemed to reflect its own brightness" (2:145).

These specimens are proffered by Altangi in a spirit of detached, objective demonstration. As items almost physically interposed between author and reader, they preclude any kind of complicity. This is of a piece with Goldsmith's dislike of literary "pertness," the style that obtrudes itself, that plays about both subject and reader in an archly familiar manner. In Letter 53 obloquy is heaped upon all writers of the "pert" class, and especially upon Laurence Sterne. "Pertness" includes triviality and grossness, and may involve bawdy, but it is chiefly characterized by a factitious intimacy that is anathema to Goldsmith: "in one page the author is to make [his readers] a low bow, and in the next to pull them by the nose." It is in the following letter—the juxtaposition is surely deliberate—that we first meet Beau Tibbs, an "important trifler" whose boast is familiarity with the great, when in actuality he has "scarce a coffee-house acquaintance" with them, and who pretends to a knowing rakishness.

Adjustment of focus and change of perspective are fundamental to the satirical thrust of *The Citizen of the World*. We habitually take short views and in our provincialism decide that what is alien is therefore barbaric. The English are fatuously surprised to discover that Altangi, a man born 5000 miles away, is yet endued with common sense (2:142). The indolent rich lady to whom he is introduced, exclaims with delightful illogicality, "Bless me! Can this be the gentleman that was born so far from home?" (2:63). So firmly rooted is complacency that when the English do acquire some knowledge, as of their European neighbors, they take the easy way of ridicule, a weakness from which Altangi himself is not free. He smugly tells Hoam: "From my former accounts you may be apt to fancy the English the most ridiculous people under the sun. They are indeed ridiculous, yet every other nation in Europe is equally so. Each laughs at each, and the Asiatic at all" (2:320).

Only rarely do the cosmopolitan allusions function simply as a kind of global color. Even when lightly applied, they have a satirical tinge: horse racing in England is "much more followed by the nobility than partridge-fighting at Java, or paper kites in Madagascar" (2:350). More pointedly, Letter 110 shows how the English could profit from the right kind of oriental imports. Ridicule of the current fad for chinoiserie moves into sardonic complaint at political parasites: "They [the English] have filled their houses with our furniture, their public gardens with our fireworks, and their very ponds with our fish. Our courtiers, my friend, are the fish and the furniture they should have imported. Our courtiers . . . would be contented with receiving large salaries for doing little, whereas some of this country are at present discontented though they receive large salaries for doing nothing" (2:426).

A nation's rites and recreations, its titles and ceremonies, will look equally absurd to the cosmopolite. Goldsmith's emphasis on broadmindedness and self-criticism, on our need to acknowledge that we are ourselves ridiculous in ridiculing those who deviate from our ways, owes a good deal to the driving force of Montesquieu and d'Argens. When in Letter 16 Altangi turns his gaze on religious credulity and enmity, he looks through the eyes of d'Argens. The positive injunction in Letter 47, however, that we should acknowledge the common ground between Christianity and Confucianism, seems to be Goldsmith's own. In attempting to comfort his son in his passionate misery, Altangi takes an antistoical line. "The truest manner of lessening our agonies is to shrink from their pressure, is to confess that we feel them." He continues: "I know but of two sects of philosophers in the world that have endeavored to inculcate that fortitude is but an imaginary virtue: I mean the followers of Confucius, and those who profess the doctrines of Christ. All other sects teach pride under misfortunes; they alone teach humility" (2:200–201). The simple seriousness does not completely conceal the slight tartness of "profess" and the repeated "sects."

Altangi is himself not free from prejudice (all nations derive their politeness from China [2:42]), and suffers from that universal human failing, vanity. This makes him susceptible to flattery and commercial persuasion, as when he goes shopping in Letter 77, where Goldsmith's comedy is at its best; since he boasts of having "sagacity enough to detect imposture" (2:69), he is predictably deceived and imposed upon. Like any innocent abroad, he takes appearance for reality. The seemingly devout congregation in St. Paul's Cathedral is in fact an audience that has assembled for the organ music alone (Letter 41). Advertisements for quack medicines, restoratives, elixirs, and the like overwhelm Altangi with their cast-iron evidence: the English are clearly so advanced in medical knowledge that they have antidotes for everything, and so generous in spirit that they offer those antidotes at bargain prices. Not surprisingly, in view of Goldsmith's medical interests and his lack of medical qualifications, quacks receive extended treatment (Letters 24 and 68). Other impostors make briefer appearances: the bogus man of learning who attires himself in the "pensive formality of slippers" (2:406), the heroes and demigods who arrogate divine status to themselves (2:446). One individual impostor, however, is fully developed: Beau Tibbs, the archetypal social pretender, a man with all the fashionable phrases on his lips, living on hopes and (invented) promises, ingeniously making the best of everything. Being accommodated in a garret, he lets his visitors believe that he is there only because of the enviable view: "We shall see the ships sailing, and the whole country for twenty miles round, tip-top, quite high. My Lord Swamp would give ten thousand guineas for such a one, but as I sometimes pleasantly tell him, I always love to keep my prospects at home [Tibbs speaks with unwitting double meaning], that my friends may see me the oftener" (2:230).

Altangi's companion, the Man in Black, has undeceived him about Beau Tibbs. But in his turn the Man in Black has revealed himself as an impostor and self-deceiver. He has erected inconsistency into a system. Embittered by his lack of success in affairs of the heart and of the purse, and by seeing the worthless prosper, he accepts the fraudulent ways of the world: it is sufficient to seem wise (by smiling and looking knowledgeable), and rich (by declining to spend) in order to be thought both these things. His autobiography (Letter 27) ends on a cynical note: "In short, I now find the truest way of finding esteem even from the indigent, is *to give away nothing, and thus have much in our power to give.*" The note would be really bitter, had we not already seen the Man in Black in charitable action. The benevolent impulses fostered by his father are too deep-rooted to be eradicated. Pretending to be hardheaded and hard-hearted, and claiming to know that all beggars are cheats, he surreptitiously relieves their wants. We can all, like Tibbs, rationalize our failures and shortcomings, or deceive ourselves about our natures and our motives, like the Man in Black, or like Altangi's son. Hingpo stoutly denies that he is infatuated by the beautiful slave girl. Of course he does not entertain "so degrading a passion" as love. Of course he feels only pity for her plight, and a deep sense of injustice, an emotion "which universal benevolence extorts from me" (2:154). Goldsmith knows well that "universal benevolence" is the most convenient and adaptable mask of all. The Man in Black's father proclaimed it the cement of society, and sheltered his own imprudence behind it; Mr. Honeywood, the good-natured man, "calls his extravagance 'generosity,' and his trusting everybody, 'universal benevolence' " (5:20).

For Goldsmith's satirical purposes Altangi has to be inconsistently both a shrewd and a naive observer, after the manner of Lemuel Gulliver. Like Gulliver, his ideals are rudely demolished, his happy anticipations turned to dust. The great exemplar is Gulliver's encounter with the Struldbruggs or Immortals. "Struck with inexpressible delight" on hearing about them, Gulliver finds the reality "the most mortifying sight I ever beheld."[6] Altangi experiences nothing so terrible, and the reader, more worldly-wise than he, does not share in his disillusionment, but only smiles at it. He is, for instance, awestruck by a group of well-dressed men, evidently "first-rate noblemen," who turn out to be an actor, a dancing master, and some fiddlers, waiting to teach dancing and deportment to a country squire (Letter 52). He visits Westminster Abbey, eager to pour out his veneration at the tombs of those who "have adorned as well as improved mankind," only to discover that a resting-place in the Abbey can be secured at a price, irrespective of merit.

At times we smile because either Altangi or some minor character is quite simply hoaxed. A practical joke will bring its victim sharply down to earth, will shatter his delusions, as Goldsmith had already shown in an essay of 1759, "On Public Rejoicings for Victory" (3:16–21). The author's "pleasing reflections" on being a member of such a "glorious political society" as England is, and the dignity and stately bearing that such reflections induce in him, are overthrown by the uncomfortable discovery that a prankster has attached a firecracker to his wig. A harsher jest is played on the impecunious author in Letter 30. Tricked into believing himself invited to meet his patron, and dreaming of a "long perspective of felicity," he finds that he has been conveyed to a spunging-house by the bailiffs. And when the prostitute takes away Altangi's watch, generously offering to have it repaired, we know he will never see either of them again. The trusting dupe prepares a joyous speech of thanks: "Where shall I meet a soul of such purity as that which resides in thy breast? Sure thou hast been nurtured by the bill of the Shin Shin," and so on (2:43). When he realizes the truth, Altangi soothes himself by reflecting that he has lost a trifle but has discovered a deceiver, and comically declares that "she whom I fancied a daughter of Paradise has proved to be one of the infamous disciples of Han." The London prostitute is unlikely to be ideologically committed to Han, but Altangi's point is sound. Cheats and tricksters, whether in China or in England, are alike under different skins. A more important point follows, as Goldsmith turns (with considerable help from d'Argens) from the cheating female to the hypocritical male. What has really fooled Altangi is not the attractive appearance and generous conduct of the prostitute, but a widespread and well-concealed immorality: "Their laws and religion forbid the English to keep more than one woman; I therefore concluded that prostitutes were banished from society. I was deceived. Every man here keeps as many wives as he can maintain," though some of them are called mistresses. The law that enforces monogamy is "strictly observed only by those for whom one [wife] is more than sufficient, or by such as have not money to buy two." English males keep up appearances in order to deceive the world at large, their families, and one another.

Altangi is likewise bewildered by the behavior of the people on the death of their monarch, George II (Letter 96). Some look dejected, others rejoice in the reign to come. In trying unsuccessfully and embarrassingly to accommodate himself to various companies of different persuasions, Altangi comes to realize that society is playing its own peculiar game. "What sort of a people am I got amongst . . . where those who have miserable faces"—the poor, who are genuinely miserable—"cannot have mourning" because they cannot afford it, "and those who have mourning"—the callous rich—"will not wear a miserable face." This movement from deception and misjudgment through social hypocrisy to the opposition of wealth and want, also appears in the most carefully engineered disappointment that Altangi is subjected to, the bishop's visitation dinner (Letter 58). Having secured an invitation to this annual event, Altangi solemnly reports the advantages of the arrangement whereby the clergy of the diocese gather at the principal priest's residence, rather than having him visit their remote parishes. Attending in the country is "quite out of the road to promotion"; if a bishop travels, he should travel to court. Assuming, somewhat inconsistently after this satirical thrust, the mantle of naïveté, Altangi pleasurably anticipates the delights of the forthcoming dinner. The bishop will naturally ask his clergy "how they have behaved and are liked; upon which, those who have neglected their duty, or are disagreeable [i.e., displeasing] to their congregation, no doubt accuse themselves, and tell him all their faults, for which he reprimands them most severely" (2:239–40). Altangi promises himself yet more edification—elevated conversation among the assembled philosophers, a Symposium with divine love as its topic. Since temperance is a Christian virtue, one can expect at this dinner "much reasoning, and little meat." The experience is otherwise. The clerics remain silent before dinner, not because they are pondering deeply, but because their heads are as empty as their eager stomachs. Once the table is groaning with delicacies they can talk only of food, and the conversation degenerates into a "rhapsody of exclamations." There is not even genuine mirth, but only crude jocularity; Dr. Marrowfat is interrupted and finally halted in his attempt to relate an anecdote of a farmer who used to sup upon wild ducks and flummery. So the reader is caught up in the web of disappointment too; this unfinished story, one of several in Goldsmith's works, is particularly teasing since it is so rich in promise, "flummery" being both a type of food (a sort of oatmeal porridge) and a piece of nonsense or humbug. With a further twist of the knife Altangi imagines another spectator of the scene, a beggar looking through the window at the repletion and sottishness within. The beggar reprimands the clerics for their gluttony and their indifference to the wants of the poor, and declares that the world censures them. The now thoroughly disillusioned Altangi allows them, in his imagination, to have the last, self-righteous and materialistic word: "What then? who cares for the world? We'll preach for the world, and the world shall pay us for preaching, whether we like each other or not."

The real victims of our deceptions are ourselves. We let ourselves be swayed by illusions, whether in unthinking terror of epidemics (Letter 69), or in unthinking adulation of shadows and titles (Letters 32 and 120). We live by clichés and slogans whose false light is so powerful that it blinds us to our illogicalities and inconsistencies. The Chinese Philosopher witnesses a scene outside a prison, where a debtor, looking through his bars, talks to a soldier and a porter who is resting from the oppresssive weight of his burden. All three are preoccupied with the possibility of a French invasion. The imprisoned debtor worries about the threat to English liberty, the porter reviles the French as slaves, fit only to carry burdens, while the soldier is fervent for Protestantism: "May the devil sink me into flames . . . if the French should come over" (2:28). Inconsistency is everywhere. The English give the impression that they are incapable of hurting the gnat that stings them, yet will whip pigs to death, or boil lobsters alive, to satisfy their appetites (Letter 15).

Goldsmith's work has often been characterized as charming and amiable. Such praise does no justice to his social concern, concern for the society of animals as well as humans. Nor does it recognize the astringency of his writing. Undoubtedly he can be amusingly playful, as when one of the club of authors brags of having produced a bit of panegyric that "would have even wheedled milk from a mouse" (2:132); the phrase sounds like something Goldsmith carried with him out of rural Ireland. His verbal catalogs, so unlike those of Swift, are lightheartedly alliterative: the finale of a modern tragedy is a whirl of "gods, demons, daggers, racks, and ratsbane" (2:93). His humor can be so unobtrusive as scarcely to ripple the solemn, even surface of the prose: "In short, the whole people stand bravely upon their defence, and seem by their present spirit to show a resolution of not being tamely bit by mad dogs any longer" (2:286). His wit, however, can also be harsh. The man who amuses a crowd by jingling the bells fixed in his cap, is "the only man that I know of who has received emolument from the labors of his head" (2:193). The history of a marriage of convenience is briefly told: "The gentleman's mortgaged lawn becomes enamored of the lady's marriageable grove, the match is struck up, and both parties are piously in love—according to Act of Parliament" (2:441). Particularly sardonic are Goldsmith's refrains. The Man in Black is unthinkingly and repeatedly

written off as someone who "has no harm in him" (2:115ff.). This harmless
individual is later made the vehicle of Goldsmith's satire on the legal profession. An Englishman, he says, likes to boast that his property is secure, and
everyone knows that a "deliberate administration of justice is the best way to
secure his property." ("Deliberate" implies both careful consideration and un-
hurried, even leisurely movement; the law takes its time.) "Why have we so
many lawyers, but *to secure our property?* Why so many formalities, but *to
secure our property?* Not less than one hundred thousand families live in
opulence, elegance, and ease, merely by *securing our property*" (2:391).
Goldsmith's discordant refrain is other peoples' governing platitude.

The letter devoted to a parliamentary election (no. 112) brilliantly concentrates many of the features I have been considering. Humanitarianism
consorts with suspicion of catchwords: Altangi is staggered at "the number
of cows, pigs, geese, and turkies which upon this occasion die for the good
of their country." Nevertheless, he enjoys the "spectacle," and mingles with
the other spectators: an election hall "seems to be a theater where every passion is seen without disguise." There is too a grim refrain, one that is still
very much to the point: "To say the truth, eating seems to make a grand in-
gredient in all English parties of zeal, business, or amusement. When a
church is to be built, or an hospital endowed, the directors assemble, and instead of consulting upon it, they eat upon it, by which means the business
goes forward with success. When the poor are to be relieved, the officers appointed to dole out public charity, assemble and eat upon it."

The poor are always victims, either cheated of what might be theirs, or
ground down by the laws that give security to those who are higher in the
social scale (2:454). Their miseries are "entirely disregarded," are not part of
the human spectacle. Yet Goldsmith does not sentimentalize them. They
can be brutally untender, treating one another "with more than savage ani-
mosity" (2:369), ill-natured and impatient, quickly roused to abuse and violence. Goldsmith's refusal to sentimentalize extends to Beau Tibbs. He
cannot live on promises for ever: "when age comes on . . . then will he find
himself forsaken by all, condemned in the decline of life to hang upon some
rich family whom he once despised, there to undergo all the ingenuity of
studied contempt, to be employed only as a spy upon the servants, or a bug-
bear to fright the children into duty" (2:228).

This increasing sombreness of tone within a single letter, as here, and
again in the account of the visitation dinner, is not uncommon. Letter 90
begins with jocular comments on that fashionable nervous complaint, the
spleen. That the Man in Black is trying to dispel his gloom by practicing the
flute while ludicrously wearing a flannel nightcap, leads us to expect some

laughing diagnosis of the sickness. In fact his misanthropic depression has been brought on by reading accounts of the "hideous cruelties" of the thief-takers, men like Jonathan Wild who exploited and then betrayed the criminal fraternity. These evil men have been "enriched by the price of blood" (2:366). That is a phrase we have met earlier: "a fellow . . . grown rich by the price of blood" (2:55), and in this second context, that of tradesmen and misers, "the price of blood" is the price that commerce is willing to pay for success. The Seven Years War between England and France (1756–63) was a trade war, as commentators on both sides of the Channel recognized. Drawing on Voltaire and Johnson, Goldsmith identified the cause of hostilities as competition for North American furs and Indian territories. On the grounds of prudence alone, in Goldsmith's view, a trading nation should not also be a conquering and colonizing nation (Letter 25). Aggression will create fear and envy and lead to a diminution of commerce, while for a nation to colonize its conquests is to dissipate its human resources; the hardiest and most enterprising will leave the mother country, where they are most needed. There are also moral and therefore weightier considerations. Goldsmith's cosmopolitan philosopher declares: "I am an enemy to nothing in this good world but war" (2:345). The conflict in Canada is unjust, and its ends purely mercenary. The colonizing Europeans have helped themselves to what was not theirs to take. "Such is the contest, that no honest man can heartily wish success to either party."[7] The human cost of these acquisitive policies could be counted on the streets of London, among whose homeless and indigent are the relics of war: the crippled sailor whose matches are purchased by the Man in Black, and the disabled, begging soldier who tells Altangi how he has fought the French in Flanders, in India, and at sea (Letter 119). He has suffered his wounds and mutilations in the cause of commerce. As a landsman with the East India Company he helped to guard trading posts and protect colonial interests; as one of the crew of an English privateer he was preying on French cargo vessels. It is not accidental that his narrative is presented immediately after the account of another trading people, the Dutch, whose merchants seem to Fum Hoam meanly avaricious, and whom Goldsmith regarded as representative of commercial nations where the powerful, enriched by trade, tyrannize over the poor (3:197; 4:100–102).

As one of the rural poor, the son of a casual laborer, the disabled soldier has earlier suffered under the tyranny of local authority, and of a social system that could clumsily but effectively rid itself of financial encumbrances. Orphaned at five years old, he is passed from parish to parish; because his father had no fixed address, "the parishioners were not able to tell to what parish I belonged." The veteran and the reader see through this pretence of ignorance to the real motives: the parishioners want no additional charges on their poor rate. Yet the veteran's straight-faced reporting of their uncertainty gives it a touch of wry comedy that is both in keeping with the character's "tranquillity and indifference" in the face of misfortune (2:458) and more effective than fierce indignation in condemning the parishioners' callousness. In the end, no one will own the boy: "it was thought I belonged to no parish at all." The solution is the workhouse, where for ten hours' labor a day he is provided with food and lodging. "It is true I was not suffered to stir far from the house, for fear I should run away. But what of that? I had the liberty of the whole house, and the yard before the door, and that was enough for me."

In his later search for employment he comes up more sharply against the injustice of the legal system. Passing through "a field belonging to a magistrate" (the property/authority nexus is established in a single phrase), he kills a hare, only to be collared by the magistrate and brought to trial as a poacher. In his own more stark and accurate words, "I was indicted, and found guilty of being poor." The Game Laws are no paper statutes. Like other laws to protect property, they are "cemented with blood" (2:44). Between 1749 and 1771 there were 678 death sentences passed in London and Middlesex alone; of these capital crimes 584 were against property, not against life.[8] The narrator is reasonably fortunate. Having spent five months in Newgate jail, he is transported to the plantations, to serve as a slave-laborer for seven years. As in the description of life in the workhouse, so here a dry and understated manner makes misfortune more real than high coloring (to use a Goldsmithian phrase) would have done. "Our passage [to the plantations] was but indifferent, for we were all confined in the hold, and died very fast, for want of sweet air and provisions; but for my part I did not want meat, because I had a fever all the way. Providence was kind; when provisions grew short it took away my desire of eating." Throughout the narrative the numerous conjunctions ("and," "but," "so") establish the simple directness of the unlearned man, while the frequent causal phrases and clauses ("because . . . ," "as . . . ," "for . . .") presenting straightforward matter-of-fact explanations, create an air of resignation, an acceptance of the inevitability of his fate and the impregnability of the system: "one man is born with a silver spoon in his mouth, and another with a wooden ladle." He is a survivor, not only because, as Altangi somewhat primly sums things up, "an habitual acquaintance with misery is the truest school of fortitude and philosophy," but also because he is no rebel. In the plantations he quietly served out his time, "as in duty bound to do."

He is compliant, but he is not a cipher, for he is sufficiently self-aware to act his part. In response to Altangi's initial inquiry about his life and circumstances, "leaning on his crutch, [he] put himself into an attitude to comply with my request." Actors and orators strike attitudes; as Robert Hopkins observes, this veteran has some "thespian talents," and seems to have rehearsed his tale.[9] Before the smallest of audiences, before even the mirrors into which Goldsmith was alleged to be always peering, we play a part. The veteran's presentation of himself to his audience is subtly conditioned by the existing social hierarchy. When he has been seized by the press-gang he is allowed to exercise a limited choice, whether to serve on land or at sea. The rules of this forcible drafting permit him to join the army technically as a volunteer, moreover as a "gentleman" volunteer. There is some satisfaction of vanity, however unreal, in being able to serve "in this post of a gentleman." There is similarly some solace to be wrung from hardship by mimicking the great. Even in a French prison (he has been press-ganged a second time, as a sailor, and his ship captured) he makes the best of things by claiming a creature comfort that his betters enjoy, by pretending to sleep as well as they do on their beds of down, and by adopting a droll style of indolent nonchalance that parodies aristocratic hauteur: "One night, however, as I was sleeping on the bed of boards, with a warm blanket about me, for I always loved to lie well, I was awaked by the boatswain. . . . 'Jack,' says he to me, 'will you knock out the French sentry's brains?' 'I don't care,' says I, striving to keep myself awake, 'if I lend a hand.'" Though he is no initiator of protest or jailbreaking, he can be stirred to activity by a sense of patriotic pride. "We had no arms, but one Englishman is able to beat five French at any time. So we went down to the door, where both the sentries were posted, and rushing upon them seized their arms in a moment, and knocked them down. From thence, nine of us ran together to the quay." Our narrator does not say directly that more than himself and the boatswain assaulted the sentries (though even those odds are distinctly better than the one-to-five ratio he has bragged about). We are left to draw our own conclusions, to smile at the vanity and inconsistency that, as Goldsmith knows, beset us all, and to acknowledge that prejudice and catchphrases may both prompt us to action and encourage us to distort the truth. Slogans certainly rise to the lips with marvelous inappropriateness. When Jack's time in the plantations had expired, he worked his passage home: "and glad I was to see Old England again, because I loved my country. O liberty, liberty, liberty! That is the property of every Englishman, and I will die in its defence. I was afraid, however, that I should be indicted for a vagabond once more."

This apostrophe to a liberty he has not enjoyed, and the allusion to a property that neither he nor "every Englishman" possessed, are present only in the *Citizen of the World*'s version of the story, which originally appeared in the *British Magazine* (June 1760) and was further modified for publication in *Essays by Mr. Goldsmith* (1765), where the veteran is made to conclude his narrative with similar stirring sentiments. He announces that he will "for ever love liberty and Old England; liberty, property, and Old England for ever, huzza!" In *The Citizen of the World* his tale ends more dramatically, with a touch of hostility that keeps the humanity of the speaker before us: "Blessed be God, I enjoy good health, and have no enemy in this world that I know of, but the French, and the Justice of Peace." The doctrine of "Liberty and Property" is what the justice of the peace upholds, but in replacing the figure of authority by the abstract doctrine when he revised the text, Goldsmith extinguished the only spark of social antagonism that he had given to his speaker. In the *Citizen of the World*'s version, the end of the narration, as Altangi hears it ("no enemy . . . but . . . the Justice of Peace") unobtrusively chimes with his introductory reflections about those who "are obliged to wander, without a friend to comfort or to assist them, find enmity in every law, and are too poor to obtain even justice."

Neither this history of the veteran, nor the "City Night-Piece" was in the original "Chinese Letters." They help to make *The Citizen of the World* more grave and somber than the "Letters," an effect strengthened by the bleak epigram, a farewell to hope and fortune, with which Goldsmith concludes the book's preface. But he is only intensifying a vein of melancholy that runs right through the letters. They end, after the marriage of Hingpo and Zelis, with a petty squabble between the Man in Black and the pawnbroker's widow that terminates their courtship. This concrete example of the trivial—they quarrel over the carving of a turkey at the wedding feast—has been given its frame of reference in the preceding, penultimate letter: "But to pursue trifles is the lot of humanity, and whether we bustle in a pantomime, or strut at a coronation, whether we shout at a bonfire, or harangue in a senate-house, whatever object we follow, it will at last surely conduct us to futility and disappointment. The wise bustle and laugh as they walk in the pageant, but fools bustle and are important; and this, probably, is all the difference between them" (2:470). Laughter will at least show us to be possessed of a sense of proportion, and will perhaps hold at bay for a while the sense of "futility and disappointment."

Pantomime and coronation; bonfire and parliamentary debate: the world offers a diversity of shows, a diversity mirrored in the variety of the letters, with their inset tales, parodies, dramatized scenes, expostulations, and philosophic meditations. Nor is the observer of the pageant, Lien Chi Altangi himself, other than various in the characteristics that his author makes him display according to the literary demands of the moment. He is naive and shrewd, prejudiced and impartial, concise and loquacious, tough and tender. This does not mean that the letters are a haphazard medley. The oriental flavor is carefully maintained throughout, Hingpo's adventures form a narrative subplot, motifs and topics recur (quacks, marriage, the literary scene, for example), while adjacent letters may be linked by subject matter (the account of Voltaire in Letter 43 exemplifies the idea of the "great character" mentioned in the previous letter), or by satirical design (Sterne is followed by Tibbs). We need not, however, exhaust ourselves in a vigorous search for unity. There is enough consistency in manner and point of view to avoid the complaint of heterogeneity. While avoiding that complaint *The Citizen of the World* positively makes a virtue of variety, for practical reasons that the penultimate letter reveals: "as every object ceases to be new, it no longer continues to be pleasing; some minds are so fond of variety that pleasure itself, if permanent, would be insupportable." For all the unusual strength of that final adjective, the sentiment is an eighteenth-century commonplace. As Margaret Doody has reminded us, the age located aesthetic delight in change, transformation, movement.[10] Like Imlac and the astronomer at the end of *Rasselas,* perhaps indeed following their example, Altangi and the Man in Black finally prepare to "spend the remainder of life in examining the manners of different countries," in studying variety.

Essays by Mr. Goldsmith

That Goldsmith recognized the temptation and the danger of heterogeneity is clear from the spoof "Specimen of a Magazine" that he contributed to *Lloyd's Evening Post* in February 1762. The essayist, he pretends to complain, is restricted to one topic at one time. The writer or compiler of a magazine—like his own *Bee*—is more fortunate: "If a magaziner be dull upon the Spanish War, he soon has us up again with the ghost in Cock Lane. If the reader begins to doze upon that, he is quickly roused by an Eastern Tale. Tales prepare us for poetry, and poetry for the Meteorological History of the Weather."[11] Goldsmith facetiously entertains the idea of making his essays, in future, "a magazine in miniature"; he will "hop from subject to subject," more a sparrow than a bee. Five brief and extremely diverse items, the bogus first number of the *Infernal Magazine*, are then offered to view.

This specimen is included in the volume of essays that Goldsmith brought out in June 1765, a collection of 25 previously published prose items, together with two poems. Characteristically, Goldsmith takes a risk. By reprinting both the "Specimen" and, as the first essay, a revised version of the opening editorial from the *Bee* ("wherever pleasure presented, I was resolved to follow"), he deliberately raised in his reader's mind the charge of miscellaneity, while offering very mixed fare, including essays on education and old age, an Eastern Tale, the "Reverie at the Boar's Head Tavern," the description of Beau Tibbs from *The Citizen of the World*, and a comically condescending account of polite assemblies in Russia. There is considerable variety of material and attitude, yet the essays do not constitute a magazine-like collection. The randomness that was noticeable in the *Bee* is avoided, both because the items are lightly bound together by discernible preoccupations and motifs, and because each individual item is substantial enough to establish an individual voice and manner. The effect is not unlike that of a collection of short stories that displays a wide range of narrative techniques. One essay purports to be the customary description, by the Newgate prison chaplain, of the life and last moments of a condemned malefactor; the joke is that this malefactor, Theophilus Cibber, has been drowned and not executed. The reader, and Cibber's acquaintance, are cheated of their expectations, expectations that are raised by the doleful refrain that "Theophilus would be hanged" (3:46–48). Another essay, adapted from *The Citizen of the World*, gives shrewd paternal advice seasoned with anecdote and animal fable (2:251–54). "Some Remarks on the Modern Manner of Preaching" (3:150–55) is a straightforward and confident presentation of the views of a traveled man who is concerned at the prevailing disrespect shown to the clergy. He has heard and seen preachers in France, and now gives well-intentioned advice to their English counterparts, in a tone that is serious but not pompous, earnest without being exclamatory. In contrast, the narrator of "A Description of Various Clubs" (3:6–16) is a countryman exploring in some bewilderment London's social scene. Here Goldsmith deploys again the Swiftian device of baffled expectations. When he is invited to the Muzzy Club the enraptured narrator adopts Gulliver's very cadence: "Happy society, thought I to myself, where the members think before they speak, deliver nothing rashly, but convey their thoughts to each other pregnant with meaning, and matured by reflection." Unsurprisingly, the members have nothing to say, because they have not a thought in their heads. The poor newcomer to London experiences yet another disillusionment.

These four essays differ widely from one another, but each is written from a single standpoint. Others create variety within themselves through inset narratives or multiple angles of vision. In "The Adventures of a

Strolling Player," closely but not slavishly modeled on two essays by Marivaux, a young man relates his life story to the companionable, kind-hearted essayist, across an alehouse table. In this little scene there is one important prop, the frothing tankard that lubricates the actor's monologue, and whose emptiness he is careful to remark upon. The essayist's role is to replenish the tankard and to listen politely. He is deliberately colorless, to offset the flamboyance of the actor narrator, with his fashionable colloquialisms and theatrical cant. His vanity takes a tumble when his performance of Sir Harry Wildair is not approved by the local authority on dramatic art, a lady who has spent nine months in London. Striving too hard, like the beginning author described in the *Bee*, he goes from bad to worse: "my laughter was converted into hysteric grinning, and while I pretended spirits, my eye showed the agony of my heart" (3:142). His eyes are attentive to the response, or rather lack of response, of the lady critic, and simultaneously betray his wretchedness. His theatrical fame has expired, and the tankard is drained.

In revising for this volume the lighthearted essay on dress, first published in the *Bee*, Goldsmith introduced a clear distinction between the essayist and the principal narrator. In the first version both the introductory reflections and the subsequent adventures in the Mall and St. James's Park are presented by the 62-year-old Jeffrey. In the second the adventures have been related to the essayist by his elderly friend. This friend is admittedly absurd, an antiquated figure in frizzled wig and muff, destined to have his amorous anticipations dashed. In his walk to the Mall he has "followed a lady who, as he thought by her dress, was a girl of fifteen. . . . My old friend . . . fancied twenty cupids prepared for execution in every folding of her white negligee. He had prepared his imagination for an angel's face, but what was his mortification to find that the imaginary goddess was no other than his cousin Hannah, some years older than himself." Once the oddly assorted couple move into the Park they are free to observe the other visitors who are in turn free to observe them. "The polite could not forbear smiling, and the vulgar burst out into a horse-laugh at our grotesque figures." Their situation is that of Altangi and Tibbs in the Mall. With shrewd insight Jeffrey interprets their growing peevishness—they begin to behave "like two mice on a string"—as an attempt "to revenge the impertinence of the spectators upon each other." It is more satisfying to take revenge on the spectators, so Jeffrey finds peace of mind by regarding the company in the park as "passing in review" before him, as though he is the distinguished visitor for whom the spectacle has been contrived: "For my entertainment the beauty had all that morning been improving her charms, the beau had put on lace, and the

young doctor a big wig, merely to please me." It is a way of solacing oneself
that we have met in *The Citizen of the World*. Hannah takes a different line.
She evidently regards other women as rivals in dress and looks, and needs no
encouragement to point the finger of scorn at the passersby. The final revelation that the Park affords is a straightforward example of hypocrisy.
Cousin Hannah scoffs, from a distance, at the overdressed Miss Mazzard.
When Miss Mazzard approaches, Jeffrey finds, "by the warmth of the two
ladies' protestations," that they are evidently "intimate, esteemed friends
and acquaintances. Both were so pleased at this happy rencounter, that they
were resolved not to part for the day." The essay fittingly ends with a sub-
dued pun, as Jeffrey "sees" the ladies into a hackney coach.

Of the two poems included in the volume, one, "The Double Transformation" (originally "The Double Metamorphosis") is particularly relevant
to the matter of seeing and being seen. Jack Bookworm, a clergyman of 36,
is smitten with love for Flavia, and hastens into matrimony. The poem
seems to be about to dwindle into a pale imitation of Swift exposing the ar-
tifices of female beauty:

> But when a twelvemonth passed away,
> Jack found his goddess made of clay;
> Found half the charms that decked her face,
> Arose from powder, shreds, or lace.
> (ll.33–36; 4:369)

This proves to be a false scent. Goldsmith's attention is not really upon
Flavia's cosmetics or her coquetry, though being "fond to be seen" she maintains a band of admirers, an audience. What interests him is how Jack's per-
ception of her physical charms is changed by his realization of her moral
failings, her affectation, and flightiness:

> Thus, as her faults each day were known,
> He thinks her features coarser grown;
> He fancies every vice she shows,
> Or thins her lip, or points her nose,

and so on, until "He thinks her ugly as the devil." Thus the first transformation. The second is accomplished by the smallpox, which intervenes to destroy Flavia's looks, and to compel her to review her conduct:

> Poor madam now condemned to hack
> The rest of life with anxious Jack,
> Perceiving others fairly flown,
> Attempted pleasing him alone.
> Jack soon was dazzled to behold
> Her present face surpass the old.

Modesty and humility, cleanliness and good nature now rectify Jack's vision, or, as he puts it, make Flavia appear really charming. Since she now displays these approved womanly qualities (the poem's standards are entirely masculine), "Jack finds his wife a perfect beauty."

To behold is to judge, whether of fashion, or acting, or good looks, or the personality beneath those looks. Since a change in the angle of vision may sometimes improve judgment, Goldsmith, as he had done in the *Inquiry*, provides such a change. Let us look at fashion and at preaching through French eyes. We may then come to a truer, that is a juster, assessment. The *Essays* certainly reinforce our sense that Goldsmith holds justice to be the supreme virtue. Indeed, the whole enterprise is ostensibly motivated by his need to do himself justice, to vindicate his legal rights in his own works; in the preface he alleges that they have been reprinted without his permission, their true parentage denied. And he wishes that justice should be done to his subjects. For example, the topic of education has been much debated, but too many writers have sought for originality at any price, have "studied to be uncommon, not to be just." We need a new treatise on the subject to set the record straight (1:455–56; this emphasis is not in the original *Bee* version). Justice should be done to pedagogues as well as to their profession; teachers should be properly esteemed and properly paid—provided that they are properly qualified, for equity demands fair play for the pupils too. Goldsmith's lengthy survey ends with an anecdote about corporal punishment in school, offering a model for the administration of justice. Since it involves trial of the culprit before a jury of his schoolfellows, Goldsmith may be felt to be a trifle idealistic. Again, the irrational fear of mad dogs unfairly gives all dogs a bad name, and leads to travesties of justice: a suspected dog will be destroyed whether it really shows signs of rabies or not, just as the customary way of trying witches ensured that they were either drowned (though in drowning they proved themselves innocent) or burnt alive (2:287). This essay concludes with a plea for gratitude, which is a species of justice, to man's faithful canine friend. The history of Alexander and Septimius, on the other hand, turns on man's injustice to man (1:363–67). It begins with the "imprudent and unjust" passion of Septimius for

Alexander's betrothed. Alexander is then accused of baseness when he has actually been self-sacrificial in love (his being "forgetful of his own felicity" anticipates Honeywood's altruism in *The Good-Natured Man*), and is later wrongfully arraigned on a charge of robbery and murder. The threatened miscarriage of justice is averted when the trial judge turns out to be his old fellow student Septimius.

Justice miscarries, however, on a grand scale in the "Reverie at the Boar's Head Tavern." The narrator, a fervent believer in the good old days of Merrie England, is instructed and disabused by the ghost of Mistress Quickly. She has seen too much for the exclamation "These were the times!" to be anything but a harshly ironic refrain. As in eighteenth-century society rich men rule the law, so in medieval times legal power and the authority of the church went hand in hand. The "tribunal of justice" before which a cuckolded husband pleads his case against a cuckolding prior, is an assembly of priests. The husband is worsted in a trial by combat (hardly surprising, since the guilty prior can appoint a doughty warrior as his champion), and is hanged "as a terror to future offenders," but only after one of his legs has been amputated, "as justice ordained in such cases." There is, as the narrator ruefully admits, nothing to choose between such ancient lawlessness and the present system, in which "a multiplicity of laws give a judge as much power as a want of law, since he is ever sure to find among the number some to countenance his partiality" (3:104). Two flagrant instances of cruel injustice masquerading as legal proceedings (the burning of Wycliffites and the execution of James Talbot) were removed from the original version of the "Reverie" in the *British Magazine*, when Goldsmith prepared his text for the *Essays*. Enough remains—the whims and tyrannies of the monarch, the deaths of the sinful prior and of Jane Rouse, both falsely accused of witchcraft—to compose a bitter indictment.

Two other essays consider aspects of justice more abstractly. From the *Bee* Goldsmith reprints "On Justice and Generosity," in the main a translation of French sources (1:405–8). Generosity satisfies our vanity, earns us respect and praise. The repaying of a debt, on the other hand, is regarded as "a mere mechanic virtue, only fit for tradesmen." This prevalent, false estimate arises from a very imperfect sense of what true justice is. "Justice may be defined: that virtue which impels us to give to every person what is his due. . . . Our duty to our Maker, to each other, and to ourselves, are fully answered if we give them what we owe them. [Several of Goldsmith's characters forget their duty to themselves.] Thus justice, properly speaking, is the only virtue, and all the rest have their origin in it" (1:406). Fortitude, if not guided by justice, can degenerate into obstinacy. Charity can warp into imprudence, if we bounteously reward the undeserving, or impair our circumstances "by present benefactions, so as to render us incapable of future ones."

Justice may be the only virtue; it does not follow that in this fallen world it can ever be absolutely upheld. This is what Asem the misanthropist learns, under the beneficent guidance of the Genius of Conviction (3:58–66). Once Asem has bankrupted himself by generous charity he finds that no one wishes to know him. Having retreated into despairing seclusion, he affirms that all nature, with the important exception of mankind, is "beautiful, just, and wise," and longs for a world without vice. The Genius leads him into just such a fabulous world, and like Goldsmith's other naifs, Asem is enraptured. We know at once that his high hopes will be dashed. To live without violence and injustice, as the Genius demonstrates, is to tolerate all creatures, however noxious. In this brave new world animals of prey therefore prey unchecked on terrified man. So we are obliged to be "guilty of tyranny and injustice to the brute creation, if we would enjoy the world ourselves." Worse still, it is an act of injustice, in a country where there is no wasteful superfluity of goods, for the inhabitants to succor a man dying of consumption, by taking bread from their own mouths to put into his. Asem recognizes that the rigid principle of justice conflicts with the claims of compassion and companionship, love of country and love of life. As the rigor of man-made laws must be tempered by mercy, so the abstract idea of justice must be compromised and modified by other impulses if we are not to lose our humanity.

The volume of *Essays by Mr. Goldsmith* was partly a commercial undertaking, since Mr. Goldsmith was now the celebrated author of "The Traveller." It is a less impressive achievement than *The Citizen of the World*, on which, as on the *Bee*, it is heavily dependent for its material. But it is not a catchpenny publication. The reprinted essays have all been thoroughly revised to produce a volume that has the same virtue of coherent variety as *The Citizen of the World*. The motifs of seeing and being seen, of justice and injustice, of credulity and experience, unite what are some of the most brilliant of Goldsmith's comedies of frustration and disappointment.

Chapter Four

Biographies

Like Johnson, Goldsmith wrote biography throughout his career. His earliest brief lives are found in the *Bee*, which contains Charles XII of Sweden, Maupertuis, and Father Freijo, while among his last periodical pieces, written for the *Westminster Magazine* in 1773, is the "History of Cyrillo Padovano, the Noted Sleepwalker." Some of the biographical writing, whether in short or more extended compass, is admittedly routine. Goldsmith himself referred to the "Memoirs of Voltaire," tossed off in four weeks during 1759, as "no more than a catchpenny."[1] The *Life of Bolingbroke* (1770) is likewise a potboiler, a rewriting, though not without flair, of the relevant article in the *Biographia Britannica*. The two works that deserve attention are one of his most polished and innovative achievements, the *Life of Dr. Parnell* (1770), and one of his most substantial and audacious, the *Life of Richard Nash* (1762). Even here the habit of borrowing persists. Arthur Friedman estimated that one-tenth of the *Life of Nash* derives from John Wood's *Essay towards a Description of Bath* (3:281). Neither in this biography nor in the *Life of Bolingbroke* is the extent of Goldsmith's indebtedness revealed. "A trifling acknowledgment would have made that lawful prize, which may now be considered as plunder" (3:426): it is tempting to quote Goldsmith against himself. He is there upbraiding the wits of the earlier eighteenth century for not giving their sources. What was for them (he believed) a matter of custom or fashion was for him something more desperate. In the early 1760s and again in the years from 1768 to 1770 he was entering into more contracts than he could comfortably fulfill. More than once he took shortcuts, his haste leading not just to plundering but to a degree of superficiality. Johnson knew that Goldsmith could absorb information very rapidly when compiling his historical and scientific publications, an operation that Goldsmith humorously referred to as "building of a book."[2] But Johnson was disturbed by the accompanying mental laxity. Goldsmith, he declared, had been "at no pains to fill his mind with knowledge. He transplanted it from one place to another; and it did not settle in his mind; so he could not tell what was in his own books." Goldsmith neither fully assimilated his materials, nor did he, in Johnson's opinion, wrestle with first principles. Boswell, not averse to tale bearing, reported Goldsmith as having said: "As I take my shoes from the shoemaker, and my coat from the taylor, so I take my religion from the priest." Johnson promptly delivered the put-down that Boswell must have anticipated: "Sir, he knows nothing; he has made up his mind about nothing."[3]

If Goldsmith was content to take his religious principles from his priest, he was certainly happy to take his theory of biography from Johnson. In the preface to *A Compendium of Biography*, an unfinished project of the early and busy 1760s, Goldsmith begins by demonstrating the advantages of biography over other forms of advice and instruction. Parents and preceptors may be severe and authoritarian. A friend's apparent impartiality may conceal his self-interest and the pride he takes in his own wisdom. It is best for counsel to be "conveyed in an indirect and oblique manner," as in biographical works, where we are left to draw the appropriate parallels to our own experience, and so to derive guidance for our future conduct. The lives of others will furnish the best lessons. Having gone thus far in evolving a vindication of biography that partly stems from his own unhappy experience of being directed and advised, Goldsmith realizes that he need go no farther: "As the use of biography, and the duty of a biographer, are so excellently set forth in the *Rambler*, by Mr. Samuel Johnson, who, from his great knowledge of the human mind, has the art of exhausting every argument, and of seeing, as it were at one view, everything that can be said on any subject, I shall give the reader his opinion, and in his own words" (5:227). After this high but not excessive praise, Goldsmith simply quotes, in its entirety and without further comment, the sixtieth *Rambler*, that lucid and powerful argument for the study of private lives.

Johnson, in his turn, was not too proud to learn from his friend's biographical practice. The life of Parnell was designed as a preface to a new edition of Parnell's poems; it is a forerunner of Johnson's *Prefaces, Biographical and Critical, to the Works of the English Poets*, and it pioneers the three-part structure—life and career; personality and friendships; literary achievement—that Johnson was to use throughout his *Prefaces*, but had not hitherto developed. Goldsmith's tripartite arrangement is not as clear as in the *Lives of the Poets*, with their typographical signposting, but it is unmistakable, and was seminal for Johnson. More specifically, Johnson graciously acknowledged that his younger contemporary's work had come close to making his own account of Parnell redundant: "The Life of Dr. Parnell is a task which I should very willingly decline, since it has been lately written by Goldsmith, a man of such variety of powers and such felicity of performance that he always seemed to do best that which he was

doing; a man who had the art of being minute without tediousness, and
general without confusion; whose language was copious without exuber-
ance, exact without constraint, and easy without weakness."[4]

The life of Parnell was undertaken as a commission for the publisher
Thomas Davies. Its fulfillment gave Goldsmith much satisfaction, as his
opening paragraph charmingly makes clear. "The life of a scholar seldom
abounds with adventure. His fame is acquired in solitude, and the historian
who only views him at a distance must be content with a dry detail of ac-
tions by which he is scarce distinguished from the rest of mankind. But we
are fond of talking of those who have given us pleasure; not that we have
anything important to say, but because the subject is pleasing" (3:407). The
word "fond" occurs four more times, contributing to what an early reviewer
of this biography perceptively called its "sentimental turn."[5] The manner
throughout is that of a relaxed, slightly emotional reminiscence; the writer is
fondly (the word is unavoidable) reviewing the life of a kindred soul, one
who, had dates and circumstances coincided, might have been a bosom
friend. We, the readers, are treated also as potential friends, as the biographer chats to us informally and unassumingly: "But for my own part . . .";
"He appears to me to be . . ."; "by the bye"; "The anacreontic beginning
with 'When Spring came on with fresh delight' is taken from a French poet
whose name I forget, and, as far as I am able to judge of the French language, is better than the original" (3:424). As befits a quiet causerie, there
is a deliberate eschewing of any summary judgment, a refusal to pronounce
a rhetorical peroration. Instead, "I shall end this account with a letter to him
[Parnell] from Pope and Gay" (3:426). The last words of the text proper are
those of Parnell's friends, two friends with but one voice and identity, jointly
subscribing themselves his "affectionate, faithful servant." There is, however, a final generous endnote in which Goldsmith returns his "sincerest
acknowledgments" to Parnell's relatives for furnishing documentary materials, and to "my very good friend Mr. Steevens [George Steevens, the Shake-
spearean scholar], who being an ornament to letters himself, is very ready to
assist all the attempts of others."

The narrative is thus framed and permeated by a sense of a community
of friends and associates, or more precisely a series of overlapping communities: Parnell and his fellow Scriblerians—Goldsmith quotes five letters to
Parnell in full, as well as an extract from Pope's verse epistle to Lord Oxford, and draws attention to Parnell's verse letter to Pope, "one of the finest
compliments that ever was paid to any poet" (3:425); the biographer and
his immediate family—Goldsmith's father and uncle both knew Parnell,
and have kindly supplied information (3:409); the biographer and those

who, without ties of relationship, have disinterestedly helped him in his project; the biographer and his subject, a poet who has given him pleasure, a pleasure that we are invited to share. Goldsmith, Parnell, and the reader jointly create this last, most agreeable of social circles, a circle that is not static because it is continually re-created and enlarged by new readers.

Goldsmith does not naively assume that simply by keeping company with one another men and women become firm friends. He frowns on Pope's "almost inexcusable" behavior in talking freely of Parnell's shortcomings as a prose stylist: "A poet has a right to expect the same secrecy in his friend as in his confessor" (3:420). He looks, however, with evident affection on the sociable relaxations of the Scriblerian group, their country excursions, the pranks and practical jokes they played on one another, their feasting and festivities. In the company of Swift, Pope, Arbuthnot, Jervas, and Gay, Parnell "was particularly happy; his mind was entirely at ease, and gave a loose to every harmless folly that came uppermost. Indeed it was a society in which, of all others, a wise man might be most foolish, without incurring any danger of contempt" (3:416). Such "follies of the wise" are sanctioned by a strong classical and Renaissance tradition, in which Horace's ode on the spring is a crucial text. There he proposes to Virgil a convivial drinking bout, in which brief folly will be mingled with wisdom; "it is pleasant, at the appropriate moment, to cast serious thoughts aside."[6] To be free from anxiety, to be diverted, was what Goldsmith sought from social gatherings, as did Reynolds, who agreed that men go into company not "with a desire of receiving instruction, but to be amused—that people naturally avoid that society where their minds are to be kept on the stretch."[7] One unhappy result of making his poetic name was that Goldsmith felt obliged to leave off frequenting those places where, as he told William Cooke, "I used to play the fool very agreeably."[8] He consequently celebrates, wherever he finds it, this ability of the wise to relax into folly. The king of Prussia "indulged such levities as plodding dunces might be apt to call folly"; Voltaire, joining his court, entered with gusto into these "harmless amusements" (3:273, 276–77). A vignette in the *Life of Nash* shows Samuel Clarke, scientist, philosopher, and theologian, enjoying a refreshing interlude of relaxation with John Locke, in a spirit of "freedom, gaiety, and cheerfulness, which is ever the result of innocence" (3:357).

The *Life of Parnell* presents a community of like-minded intellectuals and sets up the Scriblerian group as a model of social living—for men. It also offers a critical assessment of a poet whose work Goldsmith admired, anthologized, quoted, and purloined: the crudest borrowing occurs in "Threnodia Augustalis," the commemoration of the Dowager Queen

Mother that is Goldsmith's uninspired remodeling of his favorite ballad, "Death and the Lady." Death's claim to be "King of terrors" is taken from Parnell's "Night-Piece on Death," which probably suggested the title of the *Bee*'s "City Night-Piece."[9] But Parnell has a further, and perhaps deeper, interest for Goldsmith in being exceptional, not so much for his literary talent as for his temperament. "He was ever very much elated or depressed, and his whole life spent in agony or rapture" (3:409). Similar manic-depressive tendencies were displayed by the Marquis d'Argens, described in the "Memoirs of Voltaire" as passing his day "between rapture and disappointment, between the extremes of agony and bliss" (3:273). The biography of such a man could be "useful," in the accepted sense of affording a "lesson for youth" (5:227), only in very limited ways. It has rather the aspect of a case study, challenging our idea of normal behavior. So we find that Goldsmith, forsaking his didactic intentions, constantly brings out the distinctive, the unique, and the unaccountable in his subjects' lives. Of Voltaire we are told that "no man can more truly be said to have lived" (3:227); both he and Bolingbroke felt a compelling need to be in the forefront of endeavor, to have no superiors. The shorter biographies have the same emphasis on the exceptional. Baron Holberg "was, perhaps, one of the most extraordinary personages that has done honor to the present century" (1:284). Carolan, the blind Irish harper, is unequalled in his musicianship, and more intemperate than most men in his drinking (3:118–20). Robert Boyle "came as near perfection as the defects of human nature would allow" (3:45). Jean-François Regnard, dramatist, "philosophic vagabond," and traveler extraordinary, was the devoted victim of Fortune: "few there are in whom such a whimsical turn of Fate has manifested itself in the course of a short life."[10] Finally, the somnambulist Cyrillo Padovano is palpably odd. His sleepwalking self is totally different from his waking self, intellectually, socially, and morally. He is a man "of a double character" (3:214) whose divided personality associates him with two of Goldsmith's most interesting characters: Sir William Thornhill, alias Mr. Burchell, and Charles Marlow, perky with barmaids but petrified by ladies of a superior class. That Padovano, at least, is to be considered primarily as an object of scientific curiosity, is clear from the relationship between his biography (the *Westminster Magazine* essay, 1773) and the chapter "Of Sleep and Hunger" in the *History of the Earth and Animated Nature* (1774). In that chapter similar material appears, though ascribed to other persons; for the essay Goldsmith created a single sleepwalker to provide the continuity and focus that a periodical contribution requires. But the effect of essay and chapter is the same: Padovano and sleepwalkers like him show what animated nature is startlingly capable of.

Goldsmith had joked that the eye-catching title of his memoir of Voltaire, "The Life of a Very Extraordinary Man," was no more than a piece of advertising.[11] But in a sense all his biographical subjects are very extraordinary men, none more so than Richard ("Beau") Nash, master of ceremonies at Bath, the undisputed ruler of that spa for over 50 years. At the outset of this life, perhaps nervous at having dared to choose so flimsy a topic, Goldsmith once more pleads the general utility of biography, and once more buttresses his case by appropriating the words of Johnson. Whereas in the preface to the *Compendium of Biography* the *Rambler* had openly served his turn, he now silently utilizes *Idler* no. 84, declaring his serious, didactic purpose in borrowed words: "the generality of mankind find the most real improvement from relations which are levelled to the general surface of life, which tell, not how men learned to conquer, but how they endeavored to live; not how they gained the shout of the admiring crowd, but how they acquired the esteem of their friends and acquaintance" (3:290). Three years earlier Johnson had written: "The mischievous consequences of vice and folly, of irregular desires and predominant passions, are best discovered by those relations which are levelled with the general surface of life, which tell not how any man became great, but how he was made happy; not how he lost the favour of his prince, but how he became discontented with himself."[12] The origins of Goldsmith's phrases and cadences are evident, though we may note how he chooses to accentuate stylistic balance by the repetition of sound patterns: "generality . . . general," "acquired . . . acquaintance." We note too how Johnson's characteristic "discontented with himself" is replaced by Goldsmith's equally characteristic preoccupation with true and false praise, and how solitary unhappiness is changed into happy sociability. But the argument of these derivative opening paragraphs —that accounts of ordinary lives can afford real benefit to the reader in his journey through life—amounts almost to a false start. Nash is a significant biographical subject because he is an amiable freak, a man who contrived to be "pleasing to his superiors without any superiority of genius or understanding" (3:291). In himself Nash was almost a nonentity, yet against the odds he becomes material for the sort of orthodox traditional biography that Goldsmith professes to disparage, the sort that deals with the great and distinguished. For Nash was acclaimed and toasted as sovereign over his social kingdom, the self-crowned monarch of the pleasures of Bath. "Mr. Nash was himself a king. In this particular, perhaps no biographer has been so happy as I. They who are for a delineation of men and manners may find some satisfaction that way, and those who delight in adventures of kings and queens, may perhaps find their hopes satisfied in another" (3:292). The droll self-congratulation is nicely tempered by the two occurrences of the modest "perhaps" and of the polite "may."

Goldsmith has now, six paragraphs into the *Life*, put aside Johnsonian rhythms, yet without settling into stylistic uniformity. Whereas for Parnell he develops and maintains a single, appropriately sociable tone, for Nash he runs through a whole gamut of effects. Parnell was one of a steady circle of friends; Nash, to all appearances the boon companion, lived in a vacuum, acquainted with all but befriended by none. His lack of a central, stable self is mirrored in Goldsmith's virtuoso display of a diversity of styles, an avoidance of uniformity that risks instability and inchoateness. At the outset, the topics of ancestry and nurture, which the conventional biographer would handle with due respect and dutiful attention to historical sources, receive impishly short shrift: "It is a matter of very little importance who were the parents, or what was the education, of a man who owed so little of his advancement to either" (3:292). Having almost insolently turned his back on the accepted biographical manner, in the next paragraph Goldsmith deliberately parodies that manner: "to go on in the usual course of history, it may be proper to observe [the ostensibly polite "may be" slyly hints a doubt] that Richard Nash, Esquire, the subject of this memoir, was born in the town of Swansea in Glamorganshire, on the eighteenth of October, in the year 1674." For the second edition, two months later, Goldsmith solemnly added documentary proof of these statements, as befits a careful historian.

This toying with the conventions of life history is only the first manifestation of a playfulness that pervades the *Life of Nash*. It shows itself in the vivacity of the language: Nash "dressed to the very edge of his finances"; the frustrating of an adolescent love affair meant that "his happiness (or perhaps his future misery) was prevented" (3:293). When Nash commences his reforms of dress and manners at Bath, "The gentlemen's boots . . . made a very desperate stand against him" (3:305). Playfulness of a more irresponsible kind appears in the piling up of anecdotes that threatens at times to turn the biography into a jestbook, and in Goldsmith's alarming readiness to digress. Comparison with Johnson is revealing. In his *Life of Richard Savage* Johnson retails a story which, he says, "ought to be preserved," though he disarmingly admits that "it has no relation to [Savage's] life." The episode concerns Steele, in whose house Savage then lodged, and who on one occasion welcomed his guests with an apparently "expensive train" of servants. The servants were actually bailiffs; not being able to get rid of them, Steele had persuaded them to dress up in livery. Despite Johnson's disclaimer, the story is not irrelevant. It memorably conveys the atmosphere of improvidence and improvisation in Steele's household, an atmosphere that, if not exactly formative for Savage, could have confirmed him in his feckless ways. Johnson disdains to stoop to such a defense. He gruffly tells us what he believes to be the truth: this anecdote really has no direct relevance to the matter in hand, yet it "ought to be preserved," as a fine instance of subterfuge, happy extemporization, and so on. (It was fortunate for Goldsmith that it was preserved, since on this foundation he built the bailiff scene in *The Good-Natured Man*.)[13] For his digressions Goldsmith pleads not moral obligation but irresistible impulse. Telling us that he has before him as he writes a bundle of flattering letters and servile addresses that Nash in his vanity has preserved, he quotes a particularly absurd dedication sent to Nash from Taunton jail. The writer is a repentant highwayman who is willing to reveal the trade secrets of con men and other petty criminals. Goldsmith goes on: "But since I have mentioned this fellow's book, I cannot repress an impulse to give an extract from it, however foreign from my subject" (3:347). "When we talk at best of trifles," a few additional trifles are neither here nor there. The long account that Goldsmith proceeds to transcribe, of the stratagem known as "pricking in the belt," appealed to his fondness for tricks and hoaxes. It also satisfied his delight in linguistic irregularities and idiosyncrasies: "There are generally four persons concerned in this fraud; one to personate a sailor, called a 'leg cull,' another called the 'capper,' who always keeps with the sailor, and two pickers-up, or 'money-droppers,' to bring in 'flats' or 'bubbles.' " Goldsmith revels, with an almost childlike pleasure, in a variety of voices, here the offbeat cant of thieves, elsewhere the hyperbole and unintentional bathos of the journalistic laments for the deceased Beau Nash: "The peasant discontinued his toil, the ox rested from the plough. All nature seemed to sympathise with their loss, and the muffled bells rung a peal of Bob Major" (3:366). We are additionally regaled with an epigram of Lord Chesterfield's, and a not very elegant poem by Nash himself; with letters by Pope, the duchess of Marlborough, and the Quaker William Henderson; with a badly spelt missive supposedly written by the actor James Quin; with an absurdly pompous clerical admonition calling on Nash to mend his ways. If adequately diverse matter is not to hand, Goldsmith can oblige. The newspaper lament I have quoted looks like his handiwork; a letter that claims to have been sent from Nash in Tunbridge (his second kingdom) to a noble lord in London, is certainly of Goldsmith's composing.[14] The biography is a medley of styles and tones, and Goldsmith, who modestly refers to himself as its "editor," might properly be called its orchestrator and conductor.

To take such a blatantly trivial subject, as the reviewers were quick to label it, was to take a considerable gamble. Goldsmith had already justified the audacities of genius with his image of the poet on the tightrope. In this case the daring of the author matches that of his subject. Not only was Nash, like his biographer, a gamester; he also took, and got away with, immense social risks. He perfected an insolence that is a blunter kind of raillery: "Nash, though no great wit, had the art of sometimes saying rude things with decency, and rendering them pleasing by an uncommon turn" (3:356). His apparent impertinence to his aristocratic "subjects" was ultimately, as they came to see, for their own good, or at least for their good name. The duchess whom Nash cleverly obliges to donate 30 guineas toward a hospital, when she is hoping to escape by giving a mite, becomes a convert to charity and spontaneously delivers to him 10 guineas more. A lady "of no inconsiderable fortune," who thinks Nash downright rude when he tells her, in a crowded assembly, that she "had better be at home," at last takes his provoking hint and is just in time to prevent her eldest daughter from eloping with a sharper (3:322). What might seem belligerent and socially subversive is really a kind of subservience, since Nash's interventions end by furthering the interests and standing of people of quality.

Goldsmith's admiration for such effrontery is subsumed in a more sober admiration for the success of Nash's civilizing mission: "He first taught a familiar intercourse among strangers at Bath and Tunbridge, which still subsists among them. That ease and open access, first acquired there, our gentry brought back to the metropolis, and thus the whole kingdom by degrees became more refined by lessons originally derived from him" (3:288–89). There is a quiet irony in the fact that those who pride themselves on setting the social tone should owe their manners to this curiously unqualified arbiter of elegance. Goldsmith has no illusions about Nash's undereducated subjects. They need to learn their "lessons" of charitableness and good breeding. Goldsmith is sometimes content to set the learning process directly before us, as when the stingy duchess is shamed into charity, or to exemplify the corrigible fault without further comment, as when the proud duchess of Marlborough smugly but inelegantly informs Nash that her cascade at Blenheim "is a hundred feet broad, which I am told is a much greater breadth than any cascade is in England" (3:332). But when Nash goes along with his betters, drinking in their favors and applause, the narrator steps forward as social critic: "He perfectly understood elegant expense, and generally passed his time in the very best company, if persons of the first distinction deserve that title" (3:311). That Nash is accepted as sovereign of the spas reflects badly on those he rules over. For his rise to power is founded on human frailty, on gullibility and credulity. "To gain the friendship of the young nobility, little more is requisite than much submission and very fine clothes" (3:294). Once Nash has climbed the social rungs he finds that the "quality" are not above repeating his not very funny jokes, or praising his clumsy literary efforts. "Some of the nobility regarded him as an inoffensive, useful companion, the size of whose understanding was, in general, level with their own; but their little imitators admired him as a person of fine sense, and great good breeding" (3:302).

The ruler of such a vapid kingdom could easily have been presented as a caricature. That Nash, for all his own and others' absurdities, does not finally appear as such, is owing in part to the guarantees of authenticity supplied by the copiously quoted (and sometimes actually inauthentic) letters, documents, and inscriptions. More important is Goldsmith's scrupulousness in displaying Nash's real merit, the "extensive humanity" of which his benevolence is a main feature. As Goldsmith rightly says, benevolence is one virtue that cannot be hypocritically imitated or professed; one cannot easily pretend to give money away. Nash's benefactions sometimes lacked that quality of justice that Goldsmith demanded of true benevolence. They were not always directed to worthy objects, nor always untainted by vanity. They were, however, real. So were the tears he shed when he no longer possessed the means to assist the "wretched supplicants who attended his gate." Nash, in short, had sensibility, the currently fashionable quality that Goldsmith defines, quite conventionally, as "the power of feeling the misfortunes of the miserable" (3:391). Yet Goldsmith, ever wary about human motives, does not overlook the possibility that the tears of sensibility may be less than pure, may be polluted by self-indulgence: "when incapable of relieving the agonies of the wretched, he attempted to relieve his own by a flood of sorrow" (3:340).

Goldsmith's judgment of Nash is not simplistic. Neither, therefore, is the final effect of the biography. The range and complexity of the intellectual and emotional response that we are called on to make, are greater than we might have expected from so mundane a topic. "Our deepest solemnities have something truly ridiculous in them" (3:366); the generalization is validated by the pomp of Nash's funeral and all the "elegies, groans, and characters" with which the public papers mourned his passing. Conversely, the ridiculous has its solemn aspect. When Nash's death approaches, Goldsmith guards against a straightforward, simplifying reaction, whether of sympathy or scorn. After the bleak directness of "he saw that he must die, and shuddered at the thought," Goldsmith at once accounts for Nash's psychological condition by way of a dispassionate, carefully just assessment of his moral condition: "His virtues were not of the great, but the amiable kind, so that fortitude was not among the number." After that explanatory statement we are returned to Nash's state of mind; the pathos is checked by a recognition that man is both pitiably and laughably inconsistent: "Anxious, timid, his thoughts still hanging on a receding world, he desired to enjoy a little longer that life, the miseries of which he had experienced so long." Finally the tone shifts once again, as the appropriate, slightly sardonic image comes into play: "The poor unsuccessful gamester husbanded the wasting moments with an increased desire to continue the game, and to the last eagerly wished for one yet more happy throw" (3:364–65).

We have already witnessed the absurdity of the decrepit octogenarian unable to give up the habits of younger days:

An old man thus striving after pleasure is indeed an object of pity; but a man at once old and poor, running on in this pursuit, might excite astonishment. To see a being, both by fortune and constitution rendered incapable of enjoyment, still haunting those pleasures he was no longer to share in; to see one of almost ninety settling the fashion of a lady's cap, or assigning her place in a country dance . . . a sight like this might well serve as a satire on humanity, might show that man is the only preposterous creature alive, who pursues the shadow of pleasure without temptation. (3:361)

"Striving after"; "running on in this pursuit"; "who pursues the shadow of pleasure": it is the same meaningless bustle, conducting us to "futility and disappointment," that Goldsmith had contemplated at the end of *The Citizen of the World*. Humanity emerges with little credit from the *Life of Nash*. If we set on one side of the scale Nash's cheerfulness and considerateness, his generosity and charitable works, on the other is heaped the superficiality and scandal, the toadying and condescension of Nash and his subjects, their vanity, self-aggrandizement, cheating, and hypocrisy. The opening paragraph, as we have seen, echoes Johnson in its assertion that the humble as well as the great may fairly claim the biographer's attention, since all men possess the same senses and faculties. The determined cutting down to size, however, the note of harsh belittlement in that paragraph, is Goldsmith's own: "whether the hero or the clown be the subject of the memoir, it is only man that appears, with all his native minuteness about him, for nothing very great was ever yet formed from the little materials of humanity."

Chapter Five
The Vicar of Wakefield

As a book reviewer Goldsmith was necessarily a student of title pages. In one of his earliest reviews he thus rebukes the author of *Memoirs of Sir Thomas Hughson, and Mr. Joseph Williams; with the Remarkable History, Travels, and Distresses of Telemachus Lovet:* "Fair promises! Yet like a Smithfield [i.e., Bartholomew Fair] conjuror, who, to draw company, exhibits at the door his best show for nothing, this author exhausts all his scanty funds on the title page." Another work may tempt us with hints of arcane thrills: *The History of Cleanthes, an Englishman of the Highest Quality.* From its title page "some readers may be induced to search into this performance for hidden satire, or political allegory," only to find an improbable and tepidly written romance.[1] A book's title is a contract between author and reader that the former is bound to honor. Goldsmith was acknowledging the responsibility of the writer to his public, at a time when that public was rapidly displacing the patron and the subscriber as the writer's paymaster.

A title can be honest and yet characterful. In a later review Goldsmith approvingly cited Samuel Butler's maxim: "There is a kind of physiognomy in the titles of books, no less than in the faces of men, by which a skillful observer will as well know what to expect from the one as the other" (1:212). What the title page of *The Vicar of Wakefield* presents is a teasing countenance, not unlike its author's in mingling seriousness and humor. Wakefield was proverbially a "merry" town. Its vicar may turn out to be as merry as his parishioners, or conversely may be found to stand in pious contrast to them; we are kept guessing. A mild surprise follows in the elucidatory phrase "A tale; supposed to be written by himself," for eighteenth-century readers would have expected a fictional autobiography to have been labeled "Memoir," or "History," or "Life and Adventures." There is, too, an arch contradiction in the phrase. A "tale" concerning Wakefield arouses expectations of the simple and the artless, whereas "supposed to be written . . ." is an admission that the autobiographical pretence is just that; a pretence, an artifice. Our suspicion of a twinkle in the eye of this title page is checked, however, by the severity of the epigraph, from Burton's *Anatomy of Melancholy:* "*Sperate miseri, cavete faelices*" (Be hopeful, you who are wretched; beware, you who enjoy happiness). We infer that we are about to read something moral, even morally didactic, an exemplification of rising and falling fortunes. The title page promises a curious compound, which may prove on analysis to be somewhat unstable. The book has certainly proved difficult to describe and assess. A contemporary reviewer called it "this very singular Tale." Later readers have judged it a charming idyll, or a romance in miniature. Others regard it as a satire on facile Christian optimism, clerical complacency, and simple-minded faith in man's innocence. Johnson declared it a "mere fanciful performance," containing "nothing of real life . . . and very little of nature." Ricardo Quintana believes that "the real theme of this seemingly innocent book is discovery about life."[2] The elements of the tale that have provoked such critical diversity and bewilderment may be analogous to the aspects of Goldsmith's tone and expression that caused his conversational sallies to be so variously interpreted: a deadpan look can be misread as solemnity; a twinkle in the eye may be dismissed as a trick of the light.

The book's anatomy is less controversial than its expressive features. Many critics have remarked on the formal symmetries: 32 chapters divided into two equal parts, matching (though in reverse order) the two halves of the Latin epigraph. Though the first misfortune—the absconding of the Vicar's banker—is a severe blow and immediately leads to the breaking off of his eldest son George's engagement to Arabella Wilmot, the Vicar's decision to move from Wakefield to a smaller country parish, and to cultivate a farm as well as his clerical duties, permits him to keep his family above the level of poverty. They do indeed suffer various embarrassing and irritating "mortifications," blows to their foolish pride. But it is only with Olivia's rash elopement with the villainous Squire Thornhill that, as the Vicar tells us, their "real misfortunes" begin. News of the elopement is brought in chapter 17, almost exactly halfway through the narrative. The Primrose family now experiences a series of "calamities" and feels true wretchedness. Their home is destroyed in a fire, and the Vicar loses both health and liberty as he is imprisoned for debt by the vindictive Thornhill. He is informed that his younger daughter has been abducted, and that his elder daughter is dead, and he believes that he and his son George, who now shares the same prison on a charge of manslaughter, will soon follow her. In terms of the epigraph, the family has not been sufficiently cautious and prudent while in the state of pastoral happiness; in misery they may hope for the good fortune that begins to shower upon them in chapter 30: "Happier prospects begin to appear."

As Geoffrey Carnall has noted, the turning point of the elopement is preceded by one of the three poems that the novel contains, the "Elegy on the

Death of a Mad Dog." The other two poems also signal important though less momentous developments, each of which occurs at the midpoint of the two main divisions of the plot. The ballad of Edwin and Angelina (chapter 8) is followed by Thornhill's opening shots in the campaign to seduce Olivia, while Olivia's melancholy song "When lovely woman stoops to folly" (in chapter 24, ominously entitled "Fresh calamities") is no sooner concluded than Thornhill, defied by the Vicar, has him put in jail.[3]

Symmetries, contrasts, and parallels abound. The beginning and end of the novel display, but in very different lights, the Vicar's obstinacy over matrimonial matters.[4] He stubbornly and tactlessly maintains the doctrine that members of the clergy should never remarry, only to discover that Arabella Wilmot's father, the archdeacon of the diocese, is courting a fourth wife. At the end the Vicar's inflexibility over the sanctity of marriage is seen not as eccentricity but as courageous principle. He refuses to consent to Thornhill's marriage to the same Arabella because "it would be giving a sanction to adultery. While my daughter lives, no other marriage of his shall ever be legal in my eye" (4:153). The refusal of consent is actually a futile gesture, for Thornhill does not legally require his Vicar's agreement, but it is morally right. As the Vicar sees it, the marriage would be adulterous, and would certainly be a deathblow to his daughter.

Adversity has refined and strengthened the Vicar's moral character, as it also tempers his family's attitude to catastrophe. Again, a sequence of parallels and contrasts brings out the point. Life at Wakefield is not without its "little rubs": the Vicar's orchard is plundered by schoolboys, and his wife's custards are despoiled by cats and children. "But we soon got over the uneasiness caused by such accidents, and usually in three or four days began to wonder how they vexed us" (4:19). In chapter 3 the unexpected financial disaster demands that "near a fortnight" should be given up to grief. The studied vagueness ("three or four days," "near a fortnight") indicates the Vicar's slightly amused detachment from his family's excessive lamentations. When, however, the family home and almost all their worldly goods are destroyed by fire, a week suffices to restore cheerfulness, thanks to the support of neighbors and the Primroses' own efforts to withstand adversity.

The Vicar of Wakefield reveals, then, that schematic bent of Goldsmith's mind that is evident also in "The Traveller" and the *History of the Earth*. Yet the novel has frequently been criticized as something of a literary ragbag. Besides three poems, it contains the complete text of a sermon, a political harangue, the interpolated story of Matilda and her long-lost son, and a collection of satirical anecdotes in George Primrose's story of his adventures as a "philosophic vagabond." For good measure Goldsmith adds discussions of the language of poetry (chapter 8), contemporary taste in drama (chapter 18), and the shortcomings of the penal system (chapter 27).

The charge of miscellaneousness would appear to have some substance. The brief dialogue between the Vicar and the strolling player, which allows Goldsmith to denounce unthinking veneration for Shakespeare and Jonson, and to praise nature and simplicity, seems simply digressive, the author riding a hobbyhorse. The Vicar's political arguments in chapter 19, concerning equality, power, wealth, and the importance of the monarchy, also seem at first glance to have only a slender relation with the novel's development. His long speech is at least amusingly framed: the Vicar's hosts, masquerading as a member of parliament and his ladies, are in fact a butler and his fellow servants, part of the novel's large cast of impostors. More important, the kind of local tyrant that the Vicar begins by declaiming against is represented by Squire Thornhill. The reader is already aware of Thornhill's selfish cunning. The Vicar will soon feel his oppressive power. When he is taken to prison at Thornhill's instigation, he learns that in the very cell he occupies a debtor of the squire's, "no later than last year, died for want" (4:153). Thornhill is a powerful and unmerciful tyrant, and we infer that it is he, as landed proprietor, who has failed to check the decay of the county town where the Vicar is imprisoned. The town now consists "but of a few mean houses, having lost all its former opulence, and retaining no marks of its ancient superiority but the jail." Goldsmith adds, significantly, that this prison "had formerly been built for the purposes of war" (4:141); it had been the feudal stronghold of one of the warrior barons whose political descendant is Squire Thornhill. Having been the instrument of military oppression, the belligerent fortress has now become the instrument of legal oppression.

The Vicar's harangue is introduced by references to political journals; eight names are dropped by the butler in rapid succession. And the single paragraph of theatrical discussion in chapter 18 mentions eight dramatists. In each case a context of literary production and activity is quickly sketched. For the most part the digressions either concern literature itself (poetic language, contemporary drama) or exemplify a variety of literary and rhetorical forms: ballad, song, mock-elegy, sermon, political speech, brief romance. Their cumulative effect is to enforce a sense of literariness, to develop that hint about the novel's artifice that was let fall at the outset: "supposed to be written by himself." We are unmistakably reading a work of art, and the digressions, which might seem to run counter to the formal tightness and symmetry, in fact complement those highly artful features by their displays of poetical and rhetorical artistry. The effect, in D. W. Jefferson's words, is to "emphasise the story as story, to call attention to the differences between it and life, and to place it at a certain distance from life."[5]

Perhaps the clearest manifestation of authorial control is the repeated use of a single narrative device, the reversal-of-expectation of which Goldsmith was so fond. As the epigraph implies, optimism may be suddenly clouded, and pessimism unexpectedly cheered, and the novel's subsequent insistence on patterns of reversal begins to shape it into a demonstration of a single thesis: the vanity of human expectations. *The Vicar of Wakefield* has something in common with *Rasselas* and *Candide,* those excellent and recently published types of what Sheldon Sacks has called the "apologue," a work "organised as a fictional example of the truth of a formulable statement or set of statements."[6] Many of the insets or digressions share this pattern. Matilda's anguish is turned to joy, Angelina's despair to happiness. The mad dog, which dies while its victim recovers, baffles medical prognostication. George Primrose's narrative chalks up one defeated hope after another. His encounter with aristocratic grandeur is representative. Furnished (by none other than Squire Thornhill) with a letter of introduction to a "nobleman of great distinction, who enjoyed a post under the government," and having bribed his way into the great man's house, George contemplates the splendor around him: "the paintings, the furniture, the gildings, petrified me with awe, and raised my idea of the owner. Ah, thought I to myself, how very great must the possessor of all these things be, who carries in his head the business of the state, and whose house displays half the wealth of a kingdom; sure his genius must be unfathomable!" When the grandee enters, so does disillusionment: " 'Are you,' cried he, 'the bearer of this here letter?' " Ungrammatical, vulgar, and rude, the nobleman makes a hasty departure on a pretext of business, and George is left gaping.

The reversals in George's narrative, as in the principal episodes of the first half of the novel, work toward a comic deflating of vanity, a disappointing of foolish ambitions, a disabusing of credulity. Mrs. Primrose's plan of arriving at church in a more genteel way than by walking over the fields—she wishes to impress the squire's fashionable lady friends—is thwarted by the recalcitrance of the farm horses (chapter 10). Moses' return from the fair, where Jenkinson has tricked him into parting with a colt for a gross of green spectacles, is preceded by his mother's foolish euphoria: " 'Never mind our son,' cried my wife. 'Depend upon it, he knows what he is about. . . . I have seen him buy such bargains as would amaze one. I'll tell you a good story about that, that will make you split your sides with laughing—' " (4:67). We too experience the defeat of expectations (as we shared

Altangi's frustration at the visitation dinner), for at that moment Moses returns, and the good story remains untold.

The other major episode of this kind is the family portrait (chapter 16). Not to be outdone by their neighbors, who have their likenesses taken by an itinerant painter, the Primroses, obsessed with gentility, commission a "large historical family piece." Their pride is dashed when they come to realize that the painting is indeed large, for it cannot be got through the door or accommodated on any wall. It becomes a local jest, so that their vanity is made ridiculous. Worse still, it raises the envy and malice of the locality, for Squire Thornhill has insisted on being in the picture, an honor not to be refused. So now "scandalous whispers began to circulate at our expense, and our tranquillity was continually disturbed by persons who came as friends, to tell us what was said of us by enemies." The Vicar's family, which ought to be a source of harmony and good relations in the community, is the source of discord. The disastrous group portrait is itself the image of disharmony, since the individuals are presented not with an eye to the whole composition, but as "independent historical figures." Mrs. Primrose is depicted as Venus, besprinkled with jewels; with absurd inappropriateness the Vicar, in his clerical habit, is offering his Venus a tract in favor of monogamy. Olivia, who believes that her beauty gives her power, chooses to appear as an Amazon, but dressed in coachman's gear. Her seducing conqueror, Squire Thornhill, is Alexander the Great, now lying at her feet but soon to hold the whip hand, for in the next chapter the "coachman" will herself be driven off in Thornhill's coach.[7]

Although this episode introduces some ominous notes, our response, as in the other cases of purely comic reversal, is uncomplicated. When fairer promises, of innocent peace or quiet happiness, are overturned, our reactions are less straightforward. Take the scene in which the Primroses enjoy the delights of rural relaxation. "At a small distance from the house my predecessor had made a seat, overshaded by an hedge of hawthorn and honeysuckle. Here when the weather was fine, and our labor soon finished, we usually sat together, to enjoy an extensive landscape, in the calm of the evening. Here too we drank tea, which now was become an occasional banquet, and, as we had it but seldom, it diffused a new joy, the preparations for it being made with no small share of bustle and ceremony" (4:35). Tea drinking is now something of a luxury, a small but significant pleasure that more affluent people take for granted. The admission that "it diffused a new joy" is realistic and unequivocal, with the understated "no small share of bustle" adding a note of mild amusement, the Vicar's habitual condescension to the females of the family. He proceeds: "On these occasions our two little ones [Dick and Bill] always read for us, and they were regularly served after we had done. Sometimes, to give a variety to our amusements, the girls sung to the guitar, and while they thus formed a little concert, my wife and I would stroll down the sloping field, that was embellished with bluebells and centaury, talk of our children with rapture, and enjoy the breeze that wafted both health and harmony." T. S. Eliot's words on "The Deserted Village" apply here perfectly: the melting sentiment is just saved by the precision of Goldsmith's language.[8] The fond cosiness of "little ones" and "little concert" is countered by the matter-of-factness of "they were regularly served," and by the slightly pedantic exactness of "they *thus* formed." Centaury is no conventional adornment of a meadow, while "harmony" is no vague metaphor, but the actual sounds of the music. Goldsmith's careful accuracy encourages us to believe that the parents are really, and justifiably, talking of their children "with rapture."

To suppose that this sort of idyllic contentment could last forever would be foolish. This pastoral scene, like others later, exists to be shattered: the calm and sanctity of this "usual place of amusement" is rudely demolished one autumn day by the intrusion of hunters pursuing a hard-pressed stag. Squire Thornhill, seen here for the first time, brings up the rear: "At last, a young gentleman, of a more genteel appearance than the rest, came forward, and for a while regarding us, instead of pursuing the chase, stopped short, and giving his horse to a servant who attended, approached us with a careless superior air." Thornhill has perceived a more enticing quarry and begins a different pursuit. This disruptive pattern is twice repeated. When the family, together with Burchell, are having an al fresco meal in their hayfield, their peace is again destroyed by a sportsman: the squire's chaplain wantonly shoots one of the blackbirds whose song has contributed to the rural enchantment (4:52). The third scene set in this same spot echoes the first: Olivia sings to Sophia's guitar, and Thornhill once more arrives, to mark down two new victims. The deep-dyed villain now plans to abduct Sophia and to oppress and ruin the Vicar. The ruin appropriately begins with Thornhill's steward driving away Primrose's cattle. The pastoral and peaceable world of hay and cider and cattle rearing is torn apart by the predators. Stags and blackbirds, fathers and tuneful daughters are fair game to this kind of landed gentleman and his dependents. It is a nice piece of ironic justice that at the novel's end we leave Squire Thornhill acquiring new skills. He is "learning to blow the French horn"; the hunting horn is replaced by the softer-toned instrument that often provided an accompaniment to the sort of *fête champêtre* that Thornhill and his crew have repeatedly contrived to spoil.

These recurrences of the "ravaged idyll" motif reveal the hand of art. To go further, as Robert Hopkins does, and suggest that Goldsmith is artfully burlesquing the conventions of pastoral, laughing at literary clichés, is to go too far.[9] Goldsmith is perfectly willing to mock the pastoral, as in *The Citizen of the World,* but to see burlesque in these scenes is to weaken the force of the aggression that disrupts them. The rural contentment, complete with warbling blackbirds and "familiar redbreast" (4:45), is accepted, in all its conventionality, because it is about to be destroyed. Pastoral felicity is short-lived, but it shows up the callousness of Thornhill, and the crassness of the chaplain, who gallantly offers his morning's bag to the alarmed Sophia.

The novel has other conventional aspects. Eighteenth-century fiction, short and long, contains a good many seduced daughters of clergymen. When, in the second half of the novel, Goldsmith presents his Fallen Woman, we note again the accuracy of detail. Into the more orthodox symptoms of Olivia's anguish and decline—"Her temples were sunk . . . and a fatal paleness sat upon her cheek"—Goldsmith inserts something more particular: "her forehead was tense" (4:152). As for the big scene, the Vicar's discovery of his abandoned daughter, Goldsmith both heightens the pathos and gently places it by controlling our attitude toward the narrator. The language of father and daughter is intensified by exclamation and repetition, and by a shift into the second person singular: " 'Welcome, any way welcome, my dearest lost one, my treasure, to your poor old father's bosom. Though the vicious forsake thee, there is yet one in the world that will never forsake thee. . . .' 'O my own dear—' for minutes she could no more—'my own dearest good papa! Could angels be kinder? . . . But alas! papa, you look much paler than you used to do. Could such a thing as I am give you so much uneasiness? Sure you have too much wisdom to take the miseries of my guilt upon yourself' " (4:126). At this point, as the feeling threatens to become mawkish, Goldsmith moves into another key. The word "wisdom" triggers a reflex in the Vicar, and the responsible churchman takes over from the tender parent: " 'Our wisdom, young woman?' replied I. 'Ah, why so cold a name, papa?' cried she. 'This is the first time you ever called me by so cold a name!' " This is well managed. Goldsmith at once deepens Olivia's distress and makes us smile at her father's tactlessness as he mounts his high moral horse; his reaction is an example of the rigidity, the mechanical and automatic response that Bergson identified as the great source of laughter. The curious blend of sympathy and amusement is preserved in the Vicar's reply: "I ask pardon, my darling . . . but I was going to observe, that wisdom makes but a slow defence against trouble, though at last a sure one." In introducing his maxim ("I was going to observe . . .") the Vicar sounds exactly like a man of sentiment, an utterer of admirable aphorisms and fine platitudes. A habit of sermonizing is not easily sloughed off.

As the Vicar's troubles increase, as Thornhill becomes more vindictive, the melodramatic language ("Avoid my sight, thou reptile"), and the melodramatic timing ("Just as I spoke, my wife . . . appeared with looks of terror") become more evident. There is no denying that some of the reversals, engineered for pathetic contrast, are unduly prolonged. The climactic appearance of George, wounded and in chains, is heralded by whole paragraphs of misplaced hope and premature rejoicings at his safety. There is also no denying that Goldsmith shamelessly exploits the appeal of the youngest Primroses, Dick and Bill. The two boys remain obstinately outside the time scheme of the novel, perennial toddlers and prattlers, "chubby rogues," less often referred to by their names than by the sentimental appellation "little ones." We leave them seated on their father's knees, as a little earlier they have charmingly attempted to seat themselves on the knees of their old friend Burchell. One suspects that Goldsmith created two boys so that both a gentleman's knees may be picturesquely occupied; or both arms, as when their father bravely rescues them from their burning bedroom.

In the fire scene (chapter 22) Goldsmith appears to be recalling the similar disaster that deprives the hero of his home and belongings in Sarah Fielding's *Adventures of David Simple*. David's house, like the Vicar's, is a small thatched cottage, to which a legal suit has forced him to move. But whereas the cause of that fire is carefully explained, Goldsmith's blaze is quite unaccounted for. The house bursts into flames in order to enact the recurrent pattern of expectations being overthrown. Having recovered his lost daughter, the Vicar returns home full of affectionate anticipations of domestic bliss. "It was now near midnight that I came to knock at my door. All was still and silent. My heart dilated with unutterable happiness, when, to my amazement, I saw the house bursting out in a blaze of fire, and every aperture red with conflagration!" The timing could not have been more precise. "All the rapture of expectation" is yet once more cruelly turned to sorrow. The two youngest children, now referred to as both "babes" and "little darlings," helplessly lying in their bed as the flames encircle them, are the center of attention and feeling. " 'Where,' cried I, 'where are my little ones?' 'They are burnt to death in the flames,' says my wife calmly, 'and I will die with them!' " Mrs. Primrose is coarse-grained and tough—her maiden name was Grogram, the name of a hard-wearing, serviceable fabric. These qualities, that make her seem crude and insensitive elsewhere in the book, here give her a calm strength (her husband's first reaction is to collapse), and the fire unexpectedly brings out her self-sacrificing, maternal feelings, just as Mrs. Hardcastle more comically redeems herself before the supposed highwayman: "Take . . . my life, but . . . spare my child" (5:207). It is the Vicar, however, who braves the flames, snatching Dick and Bill to safety just as the roof sinks in: " 'Now,' cried I, holding up my children, 'now let the flames burn on, and all my possessions perish. Here they are, I have saved my treasure. Here my dearest, here are our treasures, and we shall yet be happy.' " That final optimism is predictably doomed to be of short duration. In the meanwhile we need not grudge the Vicar his jubilation or his manner of expressing it. When the Book of Proverbs declares that "In the house of the righteous is much treasure" (15:6), it is not referring to heaps of gold. It is not unreasonable to claim that the offspring of the righteous man may be among his treasures. In this world, as opposed to the next, even a vicar may be allowed to talk of his children as "treasures" without being guilty of materialism.[10]

In effecting the rescue the Vicar is injured, his arm "scorched in a terrible manner." Its condition deteriorates until, when he is in prison, what with the noisome air and the confinement, his strength is sapped and he feels himself sinking into his grave. These dire consequences of the conflagration exclude the spirit of burlesque. Goldsmith is not mocking the wild improbabilities of romance. We have to take the emotionalism for what it is, to accept that the episode of the fire is full of appeals for pity and sympathy (there are seven "littles" in a passage of 500 words) that are open and explicit. These straightforward appeals do not anticipate the artful tear-jerking of Henry Mackenzie's *The Man of Feeling* (1771). Even by the side of Frances Sheridan's *Memoirs of Miss Sidney Bidulph* (1761) they look old-fashioned and naive. It is significant that Goldsmith refrained from following Mrs. Sheridan in her pathetic scenes, since he took other things from her: the names Burchell and Arnold (the butler's employer), and a strong hint for the aftermath of the fire, and the Vicar's injury. Late in *Sidney Bidulph* a clergyman is clapped in prison by the would-be violator of his daughter, and suffers a palsy that incapacitates his right hand. When his daughter and Miss Bidulph (the narrator) visit the prison, the moment is affecting:

Upon his daughter's going into the room, he lifted up his eyes to see who it was: he had a fine countenance; candour and sincerity were painted on it.

My dear, you made a long stay, said he, in a melancholy voice, I was afraid something had happened to you. What has detained you?

Oh, Sir, said she, looking towards the door, I believe I met with a good angel, who is come to visit you in prison.

I entered at these words: the venerable man rose.—A good angel indeed, if her mind be like her face. He bowed respectfully.
Pray, sir, keep your seat.

The suppression of speech markers ("he said," "I answered") at the emotional climax strips the dialogue of prosaic elements. That compression, and the terse sentences, make us feel that we are catching our breath between each new, calculated assault on our feelings—assaults led by the deliberately religious language: "lifted up his eyes," "good angel," "is come." J. M. S. Tompkins has labeled this kind of writing "sophisticated simplicity." It appears intermittently in *David Simple,* and pervades *The Man of Feeling.* But these characteristic devices of sentimental fiction Goldsmith declines to exploit.[11]

Both *Sidney Bidulph* and *David Simple* explicitly relate the patient suffering of their protagonists to the archetypal narrative of reversed fortunes, the Book of Job. David Simple is almost overwhelmed by an unmitigated series of "worldly Misfortunes and Afflictions," but, like Job, he "patiently submitted to the temporary Sufferings allotted him."[12] Sidney Bidulph is "persecuted by a variety of strange misfortunes," some of which are fierce reversals: her husband is killed just when domestic felicity has been regained. She acknowledges the justice of her friend's calling her a "child of affliction," and she cries out with Job: "Why hast thou set me as a mark against thee?"[13] But the endings of these two characters are not like Job's, for they are not returned to their initial prosperity and happiness. They are uncompromisingly refused a poetic justice that would have acknowledged their virtues. Integrity and sensibility must be their own reward. Dr. Primrose, however, finds, like Job, that his latter end is blessed even more than his beginning. Released from prison, he withdraws from the celebrations and pours out his heart "in gratitude to the giver of joy as well as of sorrow."

First proposed by William Black in 1878, the analogy between *The Vicar of Wakefield* and the Book of Job has been widely accepted. Its fullest elaboration is in Martin Battestin's essay "Goldsmith: The Comedy of Job."[14] Battestin notes that Job, like the Vicar, is vain, being complacent about his own righteousness. Minor structural parallels include the messenger figures who bring the first unwelcome news to both men. Moreover, Dr. Primrose, having been informed of Olivia's elopement, having cursed the name of Thornhill (unlike Job, who refrained from cursing the man who hated him), and having been reproved by his son for thus forsaking his clerical character, recalls both the example of Christ and the words of Job: "I see it was more than human benevolence that first taught us to bless our ene-

mies! Blest be his holy name for all the good he hath given, and for all that
he hath taken away" (4:12; Job 1:21). Battestin points out that Hugh
Kelly, the dramatic rival and sometime friend of Goldsmith, praised *The
Vicar of Wakefield* for a "masterly vindication" of the ways of providence in
its apparently unequal dispensations of happiness and misery.[15] Kelly was
presumably thinking especially of chapters 28 and 29, with their weighty
didactic headings:

Happiness and misery rather the result of prudence than of virtue in this life. Temporal evils or felicities being regarded by heaven as things merely in themselves trifling and unworthy its care in the distribution.

The equal dealings of providence demonstrated with regard to the happy and the
miserable here below. That from the nature of pleasure and pain, the wretched
must be repaid the balance of their sufferings in the life hereafter.

What Kelly claimed for the novel was what was widely held to be the "mes-
sage" of the Book of Job: the seemingly unequal dealings of providence will
be redressed in the life to come; they cannot be explained by reference to the
operations of this world, but only by reference to futurity. Novels of the pattern of *David Simple* and *Sidney Bidulph* allude to Job in the same spirit as
St. James did in his epistle: "Behold we count those happy which endure. Ye
have heard of the patience of Job." *The Vicar of Wakefield,* closer to the
structural pattern of its analogue, moves beyond celebrating patient endur-
ance of calamity, into a doctrinal vindication of providence. Job's "I know
that my redeemer liveth" has its counterpart in the peroration of the Vicar's
prison sermon: "the time will certainly and shortly come, when we shall
cease from our toil; when the luxurious great ones of the world shall no
more tread us to the earth; when we shall think with pleasure on our sufferings below; when we shall be surrounded with all our friends, or such as deserved our friendship; when our bliss shall be unutterable, and still, to
crown all, unending." The sermon is given a chapter to itself, without room
for comment or reaction, almost as though it were a separately published,
self-sufficient sermon. This virtual sealing-off from the fiction gives it a special status. It is absolute and unqualified. Yet it is not entirely sealed off. It
offers the consolation of religion to the sufferer, but the consolation comes
from one who is himself suffering.

The parallels between the Vicar and Job cannot be pressed too hard. The
former is not "perfect and upright," nor is he the subject of a satanic experi-
ment. The mishaps of the first part of the novel result from moral weakness,

imprudence, and naïveté. Though the family's departure from Wakefield is in part the consequence of their banker's absconding, another factor is what Goldsmith would have censured as the Vicar's "injustice." As Eric Rothstein and Howard Weinbrot have argued, when the Vicar "made over" the whole of his stipend to the orphans and widows of the diocesan clergy (4:21), the implication of the verb is that he put his income into the hands of trustees for that purpose; his charitable contract is binding and irreversible. He is content to live on the interest of his considerable personal fortune, but when that is snatched away he has literally no income—the contract cannot be annulled—and he must find a living (in both senses) elsewhere.[16] In assigning his stipend to the needy the Doctor has been warmhearted, but also a trifle vain and self-congratulatory: "I . . . felt a secret pleasure in doing my [clerical] duty without reward" (4:21–22). Goldsmith's point is that he is failing in his duty to maintain the financial security of his family. In being generous to one group, he has been unjust to another. It is only fitting that spontaneous benevolence and vanity together should be his undoing at the fair, where the cunning Jenkinson uses those qualities to bait his hook.

It is his vanity that makes the Vicar so comically unreliable a narrator. He reports the discourse that he holds with Mr. Burchell as they travel to the new parish: "We lightened the fatigues of the road with philosophical disputes, which he seemed to understand perfectly." "Seemed" neatly conveys the Vicar's condescension, and masks his dishonesty. For Mrs. Primrose has overheard these disputes, and shrewdly adverts to them when Burchell makes an unexpected visit: " 'Bless me,' cried my wife, "here comes our good friend Mr. Burchell . . . that run you down fairly in the argument.' 'Confute me in argument, child!' cried I. 'You mistake there, my dear. I believe there are but few that can do that.' " By the warmth of his reply the Vicar betrays his earlier want of sincerity, together with his unyielding pride in his mental abilities, while with the exclamatory "child" and "my dear" he attempts to put his wife in her place by condescending to her too.

The Vicar's real weakness is less his pride in himself than his pride in his daughters. Here too he is unreliable: "Mere outside [his daughters' good looks] is so very trifling a circumstance with me, that I should scarce have remembered to mention it, had it not been a general topic of conversation in the country." The Vicar at once proceeds to distinguish the respective beauties of his daughters, specifically in terms of sexual attractiveness. He weakly connives in the various schemes to secure Thornhill for Olivia, including the shabby plan to terrify the squire with a rival, a plan "which though I did not strenuously oppose, I did not entirely approve" (4:84). In much the same way he has acquiesced in the commissioning of the family picture, and in the unworthy sneering at the rival portrait of their neighbors, the Flamboroughs: their picture has "no variety in life, no composition in the world" (4:82). Those criticisms are not attributed to an individual speaker, but are as it were uttered by the family in chorus. The chorus may be led by Mrs. Primrose and her daughters, but the Vicar sustains his part.

The lure of gentility and smartness, in the persons of Thornhill and his London lady friends (in reality prostitutes), induces the family to abandon innocence, represented by the merriment of a Michaelmas Eve's celebration at the Flamboroughs' (chapter 11). The Primroses are setting their sights higher than this sort of fun and games, but with forbearance they "suffer" themselves to be happy. As he describes the "primeval pastime" of hunt the slipper, the Vicar insensibly slides into an appropriately earthy language. He talks of catching "a shoe which the company shove about under their hams from one to another, something like a weaver's shuttle." That the Vicar should be drawn unawares into the fun is part of Goldsmith's ingenious construction of a comic scene in his best vein, one that typically hinges on embarrassment:

It was in this manner that my eldest daughter was hemmed in, and thumped about, all blowsed, in spirits [i.e., in high spirits], and bawling for fair play, fair play with a voice that might deafen a ballad singer [Goldsmith skillfully introduces another "low" entertainment], when confusion on confusion, who should enter the room but our two great acquaintants from town, Lady Blarney and Miss Carolina Wilhelmina Amelia Skeggs! . . . Death! To be seen by ladies of such high breeding in such vulgar attitudes! Nothing better could ensue from such a vulgar play of Mr. Flamborough's proposing.

The hypocritical shifting of blame is only too realistic, as the Primrose chorus positively shrieks its mortification. Like the great politician whom George encounters, these "great" ladies proceed to expose their falseness by coarse and ungrammatical language. They, not the merrymakers, are the vulgarians. But the Primroses are too imperceptive, too attentive to the outside of gentility, to be other than foolishly impressed.

The Vicar stands "neuter" (as he describes himself) in the argument between his wife and Burchell as to the advisability of Olivia and Sophia being put under the protection of Thornhill's female agents. What being "neuter" means is that he evades his parental responsibility, failing to take a firm line, or a line of any kind, but priding himself on a silly equivocation (4:65). When he goes on to silence his conscience, "by two or three specious reasons," for the unmannerly banishing of Burchell, he is on a morally slippery path. With the discovery of Burchell's letter-case, and the Vicar's compliance with the inspection of its contents, he is well down that path. Completely misunderstanding what Burchell is about on their behalf, the family sit "ruminating upon schemes of vengeance"—"ruminating" suggests pastoral, bovine innocence, but "vengeance" shows that innocence has been forsaken. The following scene presents the family at its vindictive worst, savoring—and it is the narrator's phrase—"the pleasure of approaching vengeance," plotting to entrap Burchell with a show of welcome before falling upon him with their upbraidings, their bitter fury and crude jests. The Vicar, convinced of Burchell's "unparalleled effrontery," priggishly treats his children, after Burchell's dignified exit, to a moral allegory about the shamelessness of guilt. The guilt is the family's, and their shamelessness is soon fully displayed: first with the ostentation and immodesty of the portrait, then with the open pushing of Olivia into Thornhill's way, so as to force him to declare himself. Finally, on the very evening that Olivia runs off with the squire, the Vicar's household mirth, the sign and symbol of innocence, is revealed as sadly tainted. Partway through the first bottle of the famous home-brewed gooseberry wine (famous because potent), the Vicar begins to sound like a toper: "Put the glass to your brother, Moses." He sounds like a roué when he goes on to praise Ranelagh Gardens, notorious for assignations, as an excellent marriage market. Calling for a second bottle and another song, he begins to boast of his happiness and his children's virtue. Such hubristic folly is riding for a fall. By the now predictable device of reversal, he immediately learns of Olivia's fate.

There is about this scene, as Robert Hopkins observes, a definite coarseness.[17] Goldsmith has deftly suggested a polluted high spirits, an excitement that is slightly hysterical. With this episode the Vicar has reached his moral nadir, and the reader has got just halfway through the novel. So far the Vicar has believed that, despite temporary setbacks, things have been going well; the reader perceives that in moral terms he has been steadily declining. Goldsmith now reverses these trends; henceforward we shall see the Vicar plunged into calamities, material and physical, but climbing slowly upward in moral status.

The most delicate revelations of the Vicar's shortcomings, as I have suggested, are the Vicar's own. There is evidence elsewhere, in *The Citizen of the World* and some of the early essays, that Goldsmith enjoyed manipulating a narrative in which the storyteller gives himself away, inadvertently letting slip the truth. We scarcely need Jenkinson to make the point that the Vicar is unworldly after reading that "Matrimony was always one of my favorite topics, and I wrote several sermons to *prove* its happiness" (4:22; my italics). The Vicar adds, more tentatively but still quite seriously, that "it was thus, perhaps, from hearing marriage so often recommended, that my eldest son, just upon leaving college, fixed his affections upon the daughter of a neighboring clergyman." In the same early chapter the Vicar shows himself to be superstitious, and proud, for to repeat the common saying that Wakefield possessed a parson lacking in pride, may be construed as a form of pride. A self-deceiving narrator, morally fallible and naive, is not easy to handle. For all Goldsmith's skill, there are moments when the credulity and gullibility, so well conveyed in the fairground episode, become unreal because inadequately anchored in personality. The Vicar is made to report, but made also to ignore, the warnings about Squire Thornhill's reputation. Again, Goldsmith wishes the reader to know that the disguised Burchell is the real Sir William Thornhill; we need to be assured that this god will sooner or later descend from his machine. To give the assurance Goldsmith contrives that, in his account of Sir William, Burchell should in the emotional heat of the moment begin to confuse his pronouns: "he now found that a man's own heart must be ever given to gain that of another. I now found that—that—I forget what I was going to observe" (4:30). The self-confident patrician is momentarily as confused as the unconfident Marlow, who, in his stammering interview with Kate, uses exactly the same words (5:146); but the Vicar simply fails to see the crucial revelation, even as he notes it down.

Here the Vicar-as-character is implausibly imperceptive, while the Vicar-as-narrator is in abeyance. At other times the narrator is too much in evidence, speaking with a hindsight that is normally suppressed. So he intervenes to explain the character's deception by Thornhill. As he begins his search for Olivia the Vicar is fed false information about her seducer's physical appearance and the direction the couple have taken. As narrator he admits that in his anxious haste "I never debated with myself, whether these accounts might not have been given by persons purposely placed in my way, to mislead me" (4:94). Goldsmith has sacrificed consistency of technique for a local effect. He wishes to remind us of the Machiavellian duplicity of the Vicar's adversary, because he is anticipating their next meeting, at which Thornhill arranges a commission for George, involving a posting abroad, so as to get his rival for Miss Wilmot out of the way. We are invited to savor the dramatic ironies as the Vicar pours out his gratitude to George's "generous patron" in an uncharacteristically fulsome manner, while the villain coolly laughs in his sleeve. Individual scenes in the novel are pointed, revealing, intense, but their virtues are sometimes gained at the cost of overall coherence.

The major difficulty with all fictions dependent upon a dramatized narrator, a narrator fully participating in the action, is what Wayne Booth has pithily called "confusions of distance."[18] How close is the narrator figure to the norms of the work? Is the reader's response so fully and finely controlled by the real, as opposed to the fictitious author, that there is no room for misunderstanding? *The Vicar of Wakefield* seems perversely to create confusion of distance. In his preface Goldsmith announces that "The hero of this piece unites in himself the three greatest characters upon earth; he is a priest, an husbandman, and the father of a family. He is drawn as ready to teach, and ready to obey, as simple in affluence, and majestic in adversity." This prepares us to meet someone who adds the role of paterfamilias to the attributes of Chaucer's poor parson and his ploughman brother. What it does not prepare us for is the Dr. Primrose we first encounter, guilelessly revealing himself as vain, smug, something of a crank, bossy but also cowardly, a character all too human and far from ideal. The claims of the preface relate only to the second half of the novel, where presumably Goldsmith felt himself on less secure ground, and where the occasional staginess of the language and heavy-handedness of the ironies betray a lack of confidence. The preface admits that the clerical figure whom Goldsmith has drawn will not find a sympathetic response. "In this age of opulence and refinement, whom can such a character please? Such as are fond of high life will turn with disdain from the simplicity of his country fire-side . . . and such as have been taught to deride religion will laugh at one whose chief stores of comfort are drawn from futurity." Fearing such hostility Goldsmith might well react by defensively protesting the ideal nature of Dr. Primrose.

The Vicar considered as vicar is not without his amusing weaknesses. At the beginning of the novel he prides himself on his tracts against deuterogamy; at the end, after all his tribulations, he proudly tells us that he read out "two homilies and a thesis of my own composing" to the unduly mirthful couples he is about to join in matrimony. In case we should be too severe on him, Goldsmith has thoughtfully provided three other clergymen as yardsticks. Archdeacon Wilmot is a "prudent"—that is, avaricious—materialist, with an "immoderate passion for wealth" (4:176). With scant sense of Christian charitableness he discourages his daughter from visiting the Primroses in prison, on the grounds of impropriety. When Sir William distributes 40 guineas of largesse to the prisoners, "Mr. Wilmot, induced by his example, gave half that sum." A clergyman who has to be prompted to benevolence is unworthy indeed. Squire Thornhill's chaplain is unworthy in a different way. Besides being a slayer of blackbirds, he goes along with Thornhill's smutty joking and does not challenge his assumption that the chaplain has his eye on promotion rather than the care of souls. His London counterpart is Dr. Burdock, whose fashionable doings are reported by Misses Blarney and Skeggs. His name is that of a coarse weed, something altogether different from the pretty primrose. He is a metropolitan chaplain and fashionable hanger-on, a writer of scandalous vers de société that will stick like burs to his victims.

The preface asserts that the Vicar is "ready to obey." He is certainly obedient to the law, submitting to be taken off to prison, and reproving the parishioners who wish to rescue him by force. Despite the scoffing and practical jokes of the prisoners, he is "ready to teach" and persistent with his sermons. For him to relate his own majesty in adversity, however, is a trickier undertaking, and more than one reader has found him smug and self-regarding, as in the episode where Jenkinson brings the (false) news that Olivia has died of a broken heart, and advises the Vicar that he should now "sacrifice any pride or resentment of [his] own" to the welfare of his dependents.

"Heaven be praised," replied I, "there is no pride left me now. I should detest my own heart if I saw either pride or resentment lurking there. On the contrary, as my oppressor has been once my parishioner, I hope one day to present him up an unpolluted soul at the eternal tribunal. No, sir, I have no resentment now, and though he has taken from me what I held dearer than all his treasures, though he has wrung my heart, for I am sick almost to fainting, very sick, my fellow-prisoner, yet that shall never inspire me with vengeance. I am now willing to approve his marriage, and if this submission can do him any pleasure, let him know that if I have done him any injury, I am sorry for it." (4:154)

MacDonald Emslie convicts the author of carelessness: the beginning of this passage "is one of the worst examples of Goldsmith's leaving his Vicar open to the charge of spiritual snobbery."[19] Robert Hopkins believes that Goldsmith is deliberately exposing the Vicar's "lack of humility," revealed "by his attitude that he is already one of the chosen," since he envisages himself presenting Thornhill's soul to his Maker.[20] As a clergyman, however imperfect, Dr. Primrose carries a responsibility for the purity of the souls of his parishioners. How God will regard the Vicar's soul is a different, and an unraised question. The claim to be free of pride and resentment (which is a response to Jenkinson's use of those terms, not an unprompted boast), is shown to be valid at the end of the Vicar's speech. Now that his daughter is dead, as he believes, he cannot oppose Thornhill's marriage. His willingness to apologize for any injury he has done his enemy shows a truly Christian dignity in

humility. Yet he is no plaster saint. That his moral victories are but temporary triumphs is hinted at by his syntax; the overinsistent "though . . .
though . . . yet" warns us to expect the backsliding that comes a few pages
later. When George is revealed as the latest victim of Thornhill's malice, his
father does indeed display resentment in his passionate grief, and attempts
the only vengeance in his power, that of unchristian cursing.

Prefaces are not always true to the texts they precede. If Goldsmith's
novel had fulfilled the promise of his preface it would have been a more uniform, more monolithic, and much duller book. As with the character of
Beau Nash, we have to lay side by side the Vicar's evident failings, which
Goldsmith brings out again in the final chapter, and his real merits: his
tender forgiveness of his daughter and his refusal to sacrifice her peace of
mind to his own; his fidelity to his calling in seeking to minister to his fellow
prisoners; his principled stand against Thornhill, together with his subsequent submission and asking of pardon; his resolution "*never* to do evil"
(4:128; his italics). The Vicar is a man of Christian principles who often
(though not always, for he is only human) practices what he preaches.

The rejoicing in the final chapter, being human too, is not unalloyed;
Goldsmith shades it with little piques and contretemps. But harmony and
good-nature prevail, and the novel's domestic values are reaffirmed: the
family is "assembled once more by a cheerful fireside." This last fireside is
that of an inn, which gives freer rein to conviviality. Elsewhere the hearth,
the literal focus of affectionate feelings, is emphatically a private place, even
a place of refuge from which the "censuring world" is shut out (4:132). The
fireside was Goldsmith's customary synecdoche for domestic content,
though he never worked it as hard as he does here. The preface speaks of the
"simplicity" of the Vicar's "country fireside"; the second paragraph of his
tale says of their Wakefield existence that "all our adventures were by the
fireside." The only function of their nameless and otherwise unmentioned
servant is to kindle the fire, that fire within a neat hearth that greets the
Vicar and his son on their return from agricultural labor (4:33). That the
Primrose home should be destroyed by fire is therefore particularly horrify-
ing. Less momentously, it is a bad sign when social ambition supplants domestic content, and the fire is dreaded as a spoiler of the girls' complexions
(4:56). Significantly, when in chapter 11 Burchell utters his sardonic refrain
of "Fudge!" to puncture the pseudofashionable conversation, he does so
while sitting "with his face turned to the fire"; his eyes are on the values of
the hearth, which the family is in danger of forgetting. It is Burchell too, or
rather Sir William Thornhill, who endorses those values, echoing the words
of the preface: "I have at his [the Vicar's] little dwelling . . . received that

happiness that courts could not give, from the amusing simplicity around his fireside" (4:168). We in turn endorse this endorsement. The words of a paragon must be respected.

That Sir William is a paragon, with a good deal of Richardson's Sir Charles Grandison in his composition, is not in doubt. Skilled in medicine, he knows how to cure the Vicar's injured arm. Skilled in law, he assists in drawing up his nephew's marriage articles. Setting Christian morality before the aristocratic code, he refuses, like Grandison before him, to countenance dueling. He is both generous and just as he presides over the "trial" of Squire Thornhill, and as he first rebukes the parishioners who had anarchically aimed to rescue their priest, then cheers them up by giving them money to drink his own health—two complementary tactics for keeping the humble in their places. The adjective "majestic," which the preface accords the Vicar, is given by the text to Sir William alone, when he assumes "all his native dignity," and summons George to stand before him: "Never before had I seen anything so truly majestic as the air he assumed upon this occasion. The greatest object in the universe, says a certain philosopher, is a good man struggling with adversity; yet there is still a greater, which is the good man that comes to relieve it" (4:167). Thornhill is the book's secular hero, and is endowed with secular powers to accomplish his good purposes. His word is bond enough for Jenkinson to be allowed out of prison, and his influence with his friend the magistrate will be used to clear George's name. He applies pressure on Wilmot to have the marriage approved, and on the military authorities to get George promoted. He is evidently an approved and powerful member of the establishment, with no inhibitions about using worldly power on behalf of the virtuous but unworldly.

There remains in Sir William a trace of the whimsicality that characterizes Burchell. He teases Sophia somewhat cruelly before confessing his love, and he carries gingerbread, as always, to treat the two little Primroses. Conversely, Burchell has shown dignity and a strong sense of his legal rights in the episode of the letter-book. In many respects, however, the transition from Burchell to the baronet seems less like a shedding of disguise than a transforming of personality. It is impossible to reconcile the boast that "none have ever taxed the injustice of Sir William Thornhill" (4:168) with what we first see of Mr. Burchell. In chapter 3 the latter is unable to discharge his bill at the inn. He is out of pocket, the landlord explains to the Vicar, because "no later than yesterday he paid three guineas to our beadle to spare an old broken soldier that was to be whipped through the town for dogstealing." The action is humane, but like the Vicar's making over his stipend, it incurs the charge of being unjust, and doubly so. The beadle is being bribed to suspend the operation of the law: the soldier is presumably guilty of theft, however we may deplore the brutality of the punishment. Second, Burchell's debt for his accommodation at the inn cannot now be paid. When he accepts a loan from the Vicar, Burchell admits to an "oversight" in parting with his money: it was a rash action undeserving the name of true benevolence. Yet we are soon assured, in the autobiographical sketch that Burchell/Thornhill gives, that though when he was young Sir William was foolishly and mistakenly generous, "his bounties are now more rational and moderate" (4:30). It is as though Burchell, the irrational, immoderate ego, is allowed to perpetrate what Sir William, the id, has renounced. Burchell and Thornhill are two sides of that kind of "double character" that Goldsmith later examined in Cyrillo Padovano.

In the Man in Black and Sir William Abner (3:181–82) Goldsmith had already treated the psychological type represented by the young Sir William Thornhill; he would return to it in Mr. Honeywood. These are all men of "romantic" (that is, impulsive and imprudent) generosity whose benevolence, rooted in timidity and lack of self-confidence, may prove their downfall. Such a man seeks esteem by giving; he courts praise for his prodigality because he lacks self-respect. Abner's decline begins when he ceases "to set a proper value" on himself. Young William Thornhill "had never learnt to reverence" his own heart and its impulses. So he "began to lose a regard for private interest"—a proper concern for his own good—"in universal sympathy," that seductive slogan. He loses also any power to discriminate between the false objects of charity and the deserving: "The slightest distress, whether real or fictitious, touched him to the quick, and his soul labored under a sickly sensibility of the miseries of others." Goldsmith distrusts sensibility even when it is healthy, since it can give rise to a debilitating sorrow for the woes of others that does neither the sufferer nor the person of sensibility any good. Miss Wilmot has "too much sensibility," so the Vicar kindly forbears to grieve her with the tale of his family's misfortunes (4:104). A diseased sensibility is likely to produce the melancholy brooding and early death that Goldsmith accords to Abner. Sir William Thornhill, who appears to be headed in the same direction, miraculously pulls himself together: he resolves simultaneously "to respect himself" and to restore his financial position. "For this purpose, in his own whimsical manner he travelled through Europe on foot, and now, though he has scarce attained the age of thirty, his circumstances are more affluent than ever" (4:30). If wealth can be gained by walking about the Continent, who would be poor? Sir William's experience belongs in the realm of fairy tale. George

Primrose's is more normal: "travelling after Fortune is not the way to secure her" (4:106).

Poor Mr. Burchell still goes everywhere on foot, carrying the large staff for which (as Sophia tactlessly admits) the Primroses have laughed at him. Being laughed at is something that Burchell shares with his creator, together with his enjoyment of boisterous mirth and his affinity with children. "In general he [Burchell] was fondest of the company of children, whom he used to call harmless little men. He was famous . . . for singing them ballads, and telling them stories" (4:39). To be "fondest" of their company, to emphasize their harmlessness, suggests another aspect of timidity of temper, a shrinking from the pressures of the adult world. No one laughs at the patrician Sir William, who is famous not for ballad singing, but for public spirit. He is a man "to whom senates listened with applause, and whom party heard with conviction" (4:168). He and his virtues are "universally known" (4:29). The magisterial, upright, great, and famous Sir William Thornhill is also, the fiction would have us believe, the relaxed, slightly eccentric, hay-making, fireside-enjoying Burchell. As we know from Reynolds, in real life Goldsmith found that the role of distinguished poet was incompatible with that of the easygoing, informal companion. Our sense of the discrepancy between Thornhill and Burchell testifies to the strain that such an accommodation imposes even in fiction.

In its lack of integration the Burchell/Thornhill character is representative of the book as a whole. It is less a question of the diversity of material that the novel contains—poetry and politics, confidence tricks and little fables—than that there is no single, or even dominant, manner of discourse. *The Vicar of Wakefield* is, as Clive Probyn says, "a novel of mixed modes."[21] As we are shown, in the first half of the book, the Vicar's descent into unworthiness, we are in a precisely and often very amusingly observed world of moral realism. At the same time we feel that we are reading an apologue, a schematic and unremitting demonstration that human hopes and wishes will inevitably be overthrown, that it is in their nature to be so. We seem at times to be reading an allegory, with a touch of the fairy story about it, in which Innocence and Simplicity, aided by Wise Power, triumph over Base Cunning. But we are also reading a Christian parable of "suffering and redemption."[22] It is undoubtedly to the novel's advantage that it is not as straightforward and singleminded as its own preface, and some of its critics, would make it. On the other hand, it has to be admitted that *The Vicar of Wakefield* is too protean to be fully satisfying.

Chapter Six

Public Wrongs and Private Sorrows: "The Traveller" and "The Deserted Village"

On Tuesday 13 April 1773 Goldsmith, Johnson, and Boswell were the guests of General James Oglethorpe. At the dinner table, according to Boswell, Goldsmith "expatiated on the common topick, that the race of our people was degenerated," and proceeded to lay the blame on "luxury," that is, extravagant living and the indulgence of sensual appetite. (It was somewhat tactless to introduce this subject over dinner.) Johnson would concede only that "the great increase of commerce and manufactures" that England, and London in particular, was then experiencing, "hurts the bodies of the people": long hours and bad working conditions could impair the health of those who produced the luxury goods. Goldsmith had already said as much in "The Deserted Village": "Here, while the courtier glitters in brocade, / There the pale artist plies the sickly trade" (ll.315–16; 4:299) and he was quick to retort that Johnson was simply "going to the same place by another road," admitting the deleterious impact of luxury on important sections of society. Johnson would not tamely suffer being called imprecise: "Nay, Sir, I say that is not *luxury*. Let us take a walk from Charing-cross to Whitechapel, through, I suppose, the greatest series of shops in the world; what is there in any of these shops (if you except gin-shops,) that can do any human being any harm?" Goldsmith might have objected that ginshops constituted a very damaging exception. Instead he took an apparently flippant way out: "Well, Sir, I'll accept your challenge. The very next shop to Northumberland-house [just beyond Charing Cross] is a pickle-shop." As a spur to jaded appetites, pickles are the adjuncts of gourmandism, and gourmandism may lead to the deadly sin of gluttony.[1]

Goldsmith had not always adopted so censorious an attitude toward luxury. Like David Hume, whose essay on the subject he appears to have read, he accepted that luxury "is a word of a very uncertain signification, and may be taken in a good as well as a bad sense."[2] First, the good sense. If, with

Hume, we define *luxury* as "great refinement in the gratification of the senses," then the achieving of such refinement depends on developments in trade and manufacturing. Such developments will in turn stimulate further discoveries and inventions, a general growth in the liberal arts, and ultimately an increase in sociableness and humanity. All the energies of the state, scientific, cultural, and moral, will be activated. This line of argument is followed in *The Citizen of the World*, Letter 11, where Altangi asserts that an innocent indulgence of our appetites is naturally more pleasant than a sullen refusal to be so gratified. "The more various our artificial necessities, the wider is our circle of pleasure; for all pleasure consists in obviating necessities as they rise. Luxury, therefore, as it increases our wants, increases our capacity for happiness." Luxury is an agent of civilization; the Chinese Philosopher, product of an established civilization, is its defender.

This letter appeared in February 1760. Goldsmith evidently thought well enough of the case for luxury to reassert it later that year, in Letter 82, where he repeats the claim that "sensual enjoyment adds wings to curiosity" and so leads to scientific discovery, and where he borrows from Hume the image of luxury as a potential destroyer that actually supplies the antidote to its own poison, for the sciences restrain men "within the bounds of moderate enjoyment" (2:335, 338). Meanwhile, in the second of a series of essays giving "A Comparative View of Races and Nations" (*Royal Magazine*, July 1760) he redeploys the substance, and borrows the phrasing, of Altangi's earlier letter (3:73). These essays anticipate several features of "The Traveller, or A Prospect of Society," published in December 1764. They too open with a traveler, delighting in that "spot which gave him birth," and they propose, by comparing nations with one another, to enlarge our minds and improve our customs. Comparison will inevitably make us aware of other and choicer refinements than we enjoy, and thus open the way for luxury. The same argument, unsurprisingly, reappears in "The Traveller," as the poet, surveying adjacent countries from a vantage point in the Alps, considers the difficult existence of the Swiss peasant-farmers. Their wants may be few, but their pleasures are sadly limited by their harsh environment:

> For every want that stimulates the breast,
> Becomes a source of pleasure when redressed. . . .
> Unknown to them, when sensual pleasures cloy,
> To fill the languid pause with finer joy. . . .
> But not their joys alone thus coarsely flow;
> Their morals, like their pleasures, are but low.
> For, as refinement stops, from sire to son

> Unaltered, unimproved, the manners run,
> And love's and friendship's finely pointed dart
> Falls blunted from each indurated heart.
>
> (ll.213ff.; 4:257–58)

But if the Swiss lack what luxury may bring, this does not mean that luxury's blessings are unmixed. Goldsmith had always been aware that a case could be made against it. Borrowing from the *Encyclopédie*, he had remarked in the *Bee* (November 1759) that although frugality might reduce the range of pleasure it would promote solid happiness. A taste for the delightful superfluities of life, he warned, could bring ruinous expense, idleness, and effeminacy in its train (1:441–43). In *The Citizen of the World* too the dark side of luxury is not ignored. Animals are tortured so that the gourmand's palate shall be satisfied (2:66–67), while Hingpo angrily demands whether "every luxury of the great [must] be woven from the calamities of the poor?" (2:152); "woven" reminds us of the pale and ill-paid artisans at their looms.

More important, because more sustained, but also because it marks a critical stage in Goldsmith's political as well as economic thinking, is the anonymously published essay "The Revolution in Low Life" (*Lloyd's Evening Post,* June 1762; 3:195–98). The writer has witnessed the total destruction of a rural community. The happy and hospitable life of this delightful spot, some 50 miles from London, is shattered when a wealthy merchant, having bought up the village and its surrounding farmland, declares his intention of laying it out "in a seat of pleasure for himself." He is gratifying his own senses and desires at the expense of the villagers, who have no option but to leave. "A generous, virtuous race of men, who should be considered as the strength and ornament of their country" (the "bold peasantry, their country's pride" of "The Deserted Village"), are "driven out to meet poverty and hardship among strangers." This is no isolated incident. "In almost every part of the kingdom the laborious husbandman has been reduced, and the lands are now either occupied by some general undertaker [i.e., proprietor, landlord], or turned into enclosures destined for the purposes of amusement or luxury"—not, we may observe, enclosures to facilitate improvements in farming methods. This is all too visibly the selfish and destructive aspect of luxury. These hapless villagers have been dispossessed by "a merchant of immense fortune," and Goldsmith promptly identifies commerce as the villain. It concentrates wealth in a few hands, and wealth not only fosters self-indulgence but also gives to its possessors a power that it tempts them to use and abuse. This part of Goldsmith's essay seems to be

aimed directly at the weakest part of Hume's, where he exalts tradesmen
and merchants as constituting a pressure group on behalf of political liberty.
They have "no hopes of tyrannizing over others," says Hume, since it is
against their economic interests to do so. Of necessity they "covet equal
laws, which may secure their property" (a phrase that Goldsmith had made
sardonic play with in *The Citizen of the World*), "and preserve them from
monarchical, as well as aristocratic tyranny."[3] Goldsmith has no such faith
in the political value of merchants: "Wherever we turn we shall find those
governments that have pursued foreign commerce with too much assiduity
at length becoming aristocratical, and the immense property, thus necessarily acquired by some, has swallowed up the liberties of all. Venice, Genoa,
and Holland are little better at present than retreats for tyrants, and prisons
for slaves. The great, indeed, boast of their liberties there, and they have liberty. The poor boast of liberty too; but alas, they groan under the most rig-
orous oppression." Goldsmith's final paragraph offers, without further
comment, the admonitory example favored by all enemies of luxury: ancient Rome, sybaritic and enfeebled, its strength drained away by the emigration of "the rough peasant, and hardy husbandman," lies defenseless in
the path of the invading barbarian.

R. S. Crane, who first attributed this essay to Goldsmith and gave it its
title, described it as "The Deserted Village in Prose."[4] For the poem also explicitly links foreign trade with the destruction of the countryside:

> . . . The man of wealth and pride
> Takes up a space that many poor supplied—
> Space for his lake, his park's extended bounds,
> Space for his horses, equipage, and hounds.
> The robe that wraps his limbs in silken sloth,
> Has robbed the neighboring fields of half their growth . . .
> Around the world each needful product flies,
> For all the luxuries the world supplies.
> (ll.275ff.; 4:298)

Half of the agricultural produce that ought to have supported the community and its needs is converted into cash, or exported, so that the
wealthy landowner can indulge his taste for conspicuous consumption. The
proximity of "robe" and "robbed" makes the point with sharp bitterness: the
subsistence of the villagers has been sacrificed for the silk gown worn by the
rich man when he holds court, with leisured opulence, at his morning levee.
Hume and Altangi had presented luxury as a system of self-regulating eco-

nomic, moral, and political checks. The poem presents it as a fatally addictive poison, but discovers no antidote: "O luxury! Thou cursed by Heaven's decree . . . / How do thy potions with insidious joy, / Diffuse their pleasures only to destroy!" (ll.385 ff.; 4:302).

The passionate arguments of "The Revolution in Low Life" also underpin the critique of British society presented in the later part of "The Traveller." The British set too high a value on freedom, exalting it at the expense of social unity and the ties of honor and love. The vaunted independence of these "lordlings"—the noun is effectively disparaging—brings about a condition of competitiveness and social discord (ll.339–48; 4:363–4). Those ties that should knit together the whole social fabric are replaced by "the bonds of wealth and law," which unite one group only, and unite it against the rest of society. The ambitious and wealthy, whether their riches are inherited or derived from trade, are self-serving and oppressive. They "agree / To call it freedom, when themselves are free," and the legislature uses its powers on their behalf: "Laws grind the poor, and rich men rule the law"—the point is made with monosyllabic starkness. But the indictment is not yet complete. Goldsmith now draws attention to what his earlier discussions of prosperity and luxury had overlooked—namely, how the natural resources of overseas territories are exploited for the benefit of the entrepreneur: "The wealth of climes, where savage nations roam, / Pillaged from slaves, to purchase slaves at home" (ll.387–88; 4:266). "The Traveller" was published after the Peace of Paris had brought the Seven Years War to an end in 1763. From the point of view of British commerce the war had been most successful. The imperial ambitions of France had been crushed; those of England could now proceed unchecked. Goldsmith deliberately sets his face against the postwar euphoria that, as John Sekora has argued, decisively tilted the balance of public opinion in favor of trade and luxury.[5] Goldsmith reminds his readers that trade that is based on the profitable exploitation of human and natural resources is a form of plunder.

The political danger is that the authority of the king as head of state will be undermined by the steady accumulation of power in the hands of the wealthy few:

> Yes, brother, curse with me that baleful hour
> When first ambition struck at regal power;
> And thus, polluting honor in its source,
> Gave wealth to sway the mind with double force.
> (ll.393–96; 4:266–67)

The wellspring of national honor is polluted if the rights and authority of the king, which are the guarantees of his integrity, are compromised and appropriated by a grasping oligarchy. Goldsmith's fears must have been fueled by the disputes in 1763 between the newly crowned George III and some of his Whig ministers, though no doubt Tory oligarchs were as greedy and as power-hungry, in Goldsmith's eyes, as were the great Whigs. "For my own part," he wrote in the preface to his *History of England* (1771), "from seeing the bad effects of the tyranny of the great in those republican states that pretend to be free, I cannot help wishing that our monarchs may still be allowed to enjoy the power of controlling the encroachments of the great at home" (5:339). So the poet of "The Traveller" chooses to "fly from petty tyrants"—the overreaching oligarchs—"to the throne." Or, as the Vicar of Wakefield puts it in his political harangue, the "election" of a monarch (Goldsmith prefers not to weaken his case by falling back on divine rights) "at once diminishes the number of tyrants, and puts tyranny at the greatest distance from the greatest number of people." Goldsmith never overlooks the possibility that kings may prove despots. But the greater danger is posed by the men of wealth who seek to constrain and undermine monarchy, in the name of popular freedom, for their own selfish purposes; many a pretended champion of liberty "is in his heart and in his family a tyrant" (4:99, 103).

The final count in Goldsmith's indictment of plutocracy in "The Traveller" is that the real wealth of the nation is devalued; people are now items to be commercially bartered:

> Have we not seen, round Britain's peopled shore,
> Her useful sons exchanged for useless ore? . . .
> Seen opulence, her grandeur to maintain,
> Lead stern depopulation in her train,
> And over fields where scattered hamlets rose,
> In barren, solitary pomp repose?
> Have we not seen, at pleasure's lordly call,
> The smiling long-frequented village fall. . . ?
>   (ll.397ff.; 4:267)

The argument of "The Deserted Village" is compactly anticipated here. The destruction of rural communities is in the interests of "pleasure," on behalf of the great house and its extensive estate, and the opulence that they jointly proclaim.

The impassioned climax of "The Traveller" gains its force by moving onto a new stylistic level. Its insistent questions, apostrophes, and repetitions are markedly different from the method of the preceding survey of other European nations. There Goldsmith is tentative ("And yet, perhaps, if countries we compare"), and cautiously balanced, presenting both sides of the coin: "Yet still, even here . . . ," the "here" being Switzerland; "Yet still the loss of wealth is here [in Italy] supplied / By arts"; and of the French, "But while this softer art their bliss supplies, / It gives their follies also room to rise." The judiciousness of the earlier surveys validates the passionate concern with Britain: this is no unthinking declamation. Yet if the manner has changed, the argument has not. Britain also illustrates the poem's thesis, that every nation, "to one loved blessing prone,"—in Britain's case, the freedom and independence that are prized too high—tends to mold its social and political forms accordingly, "Till, carried to excess in each domain, / This favorite good begets peculiar pain" (ll.97–98; 4:252).

The poem sets up intricate patterns of contrast and correspondence between the nations of Europe. Pat Rogers has demonstrated the cold/warm, hard/soft oppositions between the first two countries that the poet considers, Italy and Switzerland.[6] Though there are obvious differences—one people lulled into indolence by a bountiful nature, the other wresting a living from a churlish soil—there are also unexpected parallels within the contrasts. The Italian peasant exultantly builds his meager "shed" in the ruins of some ancient palace, the vestiges of a splendor founded on commerce. His Swiss counterpart is the tranquil "monarch of a shed," because in that country the absence of commerce means the absence of palaces that might have shamed and disturbed his humble home.

Holland, even more than Switzerland, represents a struggle with the environment; indeed the land is reclaimed from the sea. Ocean, pent back by dikes and ramparts, peers over these man-made shores, and

> Sees an amphibious world beneath him smile:
> The slow canal, the yellow-blossomed vale,
> The willow-tufted bank, the gliding sail,
> The crowded mart, the cultivated plain,
> A new creation rescued from his reign.
>
> (ll.292–96; 4:261)

The packing of six features of the landscape into three lines of verse mirrors the way that within a small compass the Dutch have accomplished marvels in trade and agriculture. Holland is a triumph of industry, and therein lies its weakness.

> Their much-loved wealth imparts
> Convenience, plenty, elegance, and arts.
> But view them closer, craft and fraud appear,
> Even liberty itself is bartered here.
> At gold's superior charms all freedom flies,
> The needy sell it, and the rich man buys.

Just as Britain has been implicitly warned by the example of Italy not to trust to commercial strength alone, so the case of Holland constitutes a further warning. The British pride themselves on a liberty that cannot be sustained when men are consumed by avarice. What replaces freedom, as Holland clearly demonstrates, is servitude for those left behind in the race for riches, and dull, blinkered conformity for the money-grubbers.

No one can convict the French of dullness. To characterize them Goldsmith reintroduces himself as traveler, making the crucial point about French sociability by an apt appeal to personal experience:

> Gay sprightly land of mirth and social ease,
> Pleased with thyself, whom all the world can please,
> How often have I led thy sportive choir,
> With tuneless pipe, beside the murmuring Loire?
> Where shading elms along the margin grew,
> And freshened from the wave the zephyr flew;

[Switzerland, the immediately preceding country, has a noticeable lack of vegetation, and an absence of zephyrs.]

> And haply, though my harsh touch faltering still,
> But mocked all tune, and marred the dancers' skill,
> Yet would the village praise my wondrous power,
> And dance, forgetful of the noontide hour.
>   (ll.241–50; 4:259)

The poet's lack of musical ability is insisted upon in order to emphasize the unmerited praise showered upon him by this polite people. The "sportive choir"—literally harmonious as well as being emblematic of social harmony—and the country-dancing sufficiently mark France as widely different from England, where "all claims that bind and sweeten life" are unknown, and where friction between individuals and groups threatens either to bring the social system to a halt or to set it aflame (ll.342 ff.). But in the analytical paragraph that follows the mirthful scene, Goldsmith suggests the incipient dangers in the French scale of values:

> So blest a life these thoughtless realms display,
> Thus idly busy rolls their world away;
> Theirs are those arts that mind to mind endear,
> For honor forms the social temper here.
> Honor, that praise which real merit gains,
> Or even imaginary worth obtains,
> Here passes current; paid from hand to hand,
> It shifts in splendid traffic round the land:
> From courts to camps, to cottages it strays,
> And all are taught an avarice of praise.
> They please, are pleased, they give to get esteem,
> Till, seeming blest, they grow to what they seem.

The lines illustrate at once the limitations and the strengths of Goldsmith's verse. His couplets have neither the spring and energy of Pope's, nor the solidity of Johnson's; the lines, in their end-stopped uniformity and unassuming plainness, sometimes read flatly. Yet he can surprise by a sudden checking of pace ("Here passes current;"), or by a complex rhythmical balance and assonantal repetition, as in the final couplet, which economically suggests the self-complacent and ingrown condition of these social transactions. Again, though some of Goldsmith's verbs are conventional ("rolls away") or inert ("obtains" seems to be there only for the rhyme), the majority are working hard if unobtrusively. "Endear," in the second couplet, carries a strong emotional charge; "strays," with its suggestion in this context of haphazard, leisurely strolling, conveys the rather too genial, easygoing way in which honor circulates through the country. "It shifts in splendid traffic" is strikingly audacious, since the verb shocks by its lack of dignity; its effect is immediately to cheapen "splendid," which is further demeaned by "traffic." Honor, thus shuffled from hand to hand, begins to lose its gloss, becomes commercialized and therefore tainted, nothing more than an "avarice of praise." The French "give to get esteem"; the second verb indicates just how sordidly grasping they are.

"I have endeavored to show," says Goldsmith in the dedication to the poem, "that there may be equal happiness in states that are differently governed from our own; that every state has a particular principle of happiness, and that this principle in each may be carried to a mischievous excess." As an effort of the "philosophic mind" (l.39) to determine the true point of happiness, the poem aligns itself with Pope's *Essay on Man*. In examining the detailed effects of climate, temperament, and forms of social and political organization on the happiness of individual nations, it claims kinship with (and borrows some phrases from) Addison's *Letter from Italy*, though at the same time it offers a critique of Addison's easy patriotism and praise of British liberty. It is an ambitious, large-scale undertaking, a genuine "Prospect of Society," as the poem's original title, later its subtitle, asserts.

The poem's title, however, became "The Traveller"; the grand survey of nations is preceded by the direct expression of personal concerns, the poet's own anguished search for happiness. As in "The Deserted Village," a thesis is given urgency by a framing and archetypal motif: there the homecoming, here the quest. Goldsmith, in dedicating "The Traveller" to his brother Henry, reminds him that he had sent him a portion of it from Switzerland when on his pedestrian grand tour. In its final form the poem can be considered, as one of its first reviewers suggested, as a verse epistle addressed to Henry.[7] Like the epistolary poems of Dryden and Pope it uses its addressee to supply a point of reference, a standard of morality and conduct, a desirable and achievable pattern of happiness. Undistracted by ambition, Henry has chosen the humble life of the rural clergyman, happy not only in his sacred office but also in marriage and domesticity. As the poet envisages Henry's home, the emphasis is on hospitality and innocent mirth. From his example his family learns "the luxury of doing good," and this sort of moral "luxury" stands as a rebuke to the "sensual bliss" and delight in "superfluous treasure" that the poem proceeds to catalog.

If his brother has found felicity, the poet has not. "Remote, unfriended, melancholy, slow," he wanders through Europe, ostensibly seeking that "spot to real happiness consigned, / Where my worn soul, each wandering hope at rest / May gather bliss to see my fellows blest" (ll.60–62; 4:251). If he could only locate this milieu of contentment he would settle into it; hence the survey of nations. But the anguish of the opening lines seems to have less to do with a failure to find happiness than with the misery of being condemned to solitude, being "unfriended" and "alone." The poet is a "houseless stranger," brutally barred from shelter by the rude Carinthian boor, who is Henry's inhospitable opposite. Even more painfully he is excluded from the family circle. The use of the word "spot" for both Henry's home (l.13) and the place where the poet wishes to settle (ll.30, 60) indicates that the latter's search is essentially for a modest domestic bliss: he is not destined to share "such delights" as Henry enjoys.

The poet is "melancholy" and "slow" in his travels both because his search for happiness is admittedly vain, and because his condition is that of a sad exile, remote from family and friends. In its first version the poem apparently ended with another exile from rural Britain, a "pilgrim" who strays (the verb now suggests hopeless, aimless wandering) through the North American forests:

> The famished exile bends beneath his woe,
> And faintly, fainter, fainter seems to go;
> Casts a fond look where Britain's shores recline,
> And gives his griefs to sympathize with mine.[8]

As pilgrims the poet and the emigrant are outcasts, united by sympathetic grief, who yet persevere in the forlorn quest for delusive happiness. Indignation at the ambition and greed that has driven the villagers into exile is submerged beneath the nostalgic yearning, the sorrow, and the enervation.

Goldsmith's revision of the poem's conclusion was materially assisted by Johnson, who, to begin with, rewrote his friend's wilting line as "To stop too fearful, and too faint to go." He may also have suggested an intensification of the political note: "Casts a long look where England's glories shine / And bids his bosom sympathize with mine." The couplet has a political dimension that its predecessor lacked; England's "glories" are seen in an ironic light, and they are specifically England's: commercial power and domineering opulence are principally displayed in one part only of the British Isles. The penultimate verse paragraph now concludes with a blend of homesickness (a "long look" could mean a "longing look"),[9] generalized regret, and a touch of scornful rebuke.

The poem might have ended there; what survives of the "Prospect of Society" has nothing that corresponds with the final verse paragraph of "The Traveller," 8 of whose 16 lines were contributed by Johnson. Had it so ended it would emotionally have come full circle. But such an end to the poem would have provided no end to the quest, no solution to the problem of personal happiness. With something of an air of pulling himself together, the poet, with Johnson's help, proposes a solution. As at the beginning of the poem the unfriended, wandering poet turns fondly to contemplate his brother's serene existence, so now, after the pilgrim exile's woes, comes the realization that true happiness does indeed reside in domestic life. The two final verse paragraphs deliberately follow the pattern of the two opening ones; we have intellectually come full circle too (I have italicized the lines that Johnson acknowledged as his):

> Vain, very vain, my weary search to find
> That bliss which only centers in the mind.
> Why have I strayed, from pleasure and repose,
> To seek a good each government bestows?
> In every government, though terrors reign,
> Though tyrant kings, or tyrant laws restrain,
> *How small, of all that human hearts endure,*
> *That part which laws or kings can cause or cure.*
> *Still to ourselves in every place consigned,*
> *Our own felicity we make or find;*
> *With secret course, which no loud storms annoy,*
> *Glides the smooth current of domestic joy.*
> The lifted axe, the agonizing wheel,
> Luke's iron crown, and Damien's bed of steel,
> *To men remote from power but rarely known,*
> *Leave reason, faith, and conscience all our own.*

What is startlingly out of key here is Goldsmith's own final couplet, with its sense of menace, its pain, its specificity of reference. The two historical personages—the only such in the entire poem—bring with them a reality of physical suffering that is new and profoundly disturbing. The iron crown that was mockingly placed on the head of the captured Hungarian peasant leader was of red-hot metal. Damien's "bed of steel" was the rack on which, as Goldsmith believed, the would-be assassin of Louis XV had been tortured. The couplet is too highly charged for its context; its over emphasis and appeal to extreme cases betray the fact that Goldsmith does not quite believe in the doctrine that Johnson is imposing on his poem, and that he is doing his best to uphold. The evidence presented in the preceding 400 lines does not justify the poem's assured and reassuring conclusion. What the diagnosis of European ills has revealed cannot be adequately treated with a prescription of self-reliance and individual responsibility. In Italy, so Goldsmith alleges, "each nobler aim" of the inhabitants has been "repressed by long control," by the crushing domination exercised by powerful commercial interests. In France, for all the mirth and festivity, indeed because of the unremitting pressure to be gregarious and sociable, the individual soul remains unblest "within itself." This social climate makes self-reliance almost impossible. In Holland, "a land of tyrants, and a den of slaves," the poor and downtrodden have no recourse but to "seek dishonorable graves." Finally, in England, as growing wealth gathers legislative power to itself, it protects its acquisitions by new penal statutes that bear down on the poor alone, or establishes its supremacy by driving men and women from their homes. So many citizens of Europe, people who thought themselves remote from power, have experienced the shattering or eroding of their domestic joy by precisely those forces—tyrant kings and tyrant laws—that the poem now seeks to relegate to the wings. Its conclusion does not admit the gloomy determinism that has gone before, or misrepresents it: the poet now blames himself for having willfully strayed "from pleasure and repose," whereas earlier he had spoken of being "not destined" to share his brother's domestic delights, of being impelled by fate or led by fortune to wander alone through the world (ll.23 ff.). As in real life Goldsmith's outbursts of self-pity and of raw feeling were met by Johnson with surprise or disapproval, so in the poem Johnson's steady independence of mind cannot harmonize with Goldsmith's unashamed emotionalism, his susceptibility to external influences, his rather gloomy fatalism. The more modest assistance that Johnson provided in the case of "The Deserted Village" was to be more successful.

"The Deserted Village" was published in May 1770. Its dedication, to Sir Joshua Reynolds, speaks of the author's firsthand inquiries into rural depopulation, inquiries undertaken during country excursions over "four or five years," though, as we have seen, the topic had been on Goldsmith's mind for twice that length of time. The dedication is categorical. Villages *are* being deserted, and the reasons are not far to seek: "In regretting the depopulation of the country, I inveigh against the increase of our luxuries. . . . For twenty of thirty years past, it has been the fashion to consider luxury as one of the greatest national advantages, and all the wisdom of antiquity in that particular, as erroneous. Still, however, I must remain a professed ancient on that head, and continue to think those luxuries prejudicial to states, by which so many vices are introduced, and so many kingdoms have been undone" (4:286). As a devotee of the wisdom of antiquity, Goldsmith places himself on the side of Pliny and Cicero, Juvenal and Horace. Their advocacy of plain living and sturdy independence was ignored; the decadent sloth that began to corrupt Roman society led inexorably to its downfall.

Characteristically, because he is addressing a friend, the final sentence of the dedication puts its tongue in its cheek: "Indeed, so much has been poured out of late on the other side of the question, that, merely for the sake of novelty and variety, one would sometimes wish to be in the right." The poem itself, though not devoid of humor, has no time for such quips. "Where wealth accumulates," there "men decay" (l.52), for wealth means power, the power to "grasp" and to tyrannize, to commandeer and to evict. The poor villager who drives his flock to the scanty pastures of unfenced common land, now finds that "Those fenceless fields the sons of wealth divide, / And even the bare-worn common is denied" (ll.307–8). The newly built mansion of the "man of wealth and pride," with its newly extended grounds, "Indignant spurns the cottage from the green," as though contumeliously kicking the village community from its traditional locale. In the same way the great man's doorkeeper, brutally imitating a brutal master, "spurns" imploring famine from his master's gate (ll.105–6). Enclosing commons, turning agricultural land into unproductive pleasure grounds, and, most flagrantly, uprooting whole villages to create space for mansions and parkland, are all blatant assertions of selfish power. The blame, as in "The Revolution in Low Life," is squarely placed on commerce, on "trade's unfeeling train." These acquisitive and insensitive merchants, their profits made by trafficking in luxury goods, "usurp the land"—they do not have the interests of agriculture or the well-being of farmers at heart—"and dispossess the swain."

The swain has only two choices: flight to the city, or emigration. London presents a concentration of luxury and profusion, a place where "ten thousand baneful arts" are "combined / To pamper luxury, and thin mankind." Mankind is thinned by disease, especially among those who produce the finery, by starvation, and by public executions: "Here, while the proud their long-drawn pomp display, / There the black gibbet glooms beside the way" (ll.317–18; 4:299). Some of those who seek a livelihood in the metropolis will be tempted into crime by the ostentatious wealth around them, and will end on the gallows, shamefully gibbeted.

The villagers of Auburn are imagined as taking the other alternative, as wandering in exile amidst the torrid and desolate wilds of North America:

> Far different there from all that charmed before,
> The various terrors of that horrid shore.
> Those blazing suns that dart a downward ray,
> And fiercely shed intolerable day;
> Those matted woods where birds forget to sing,
> But silent bats in drowsy clusters cling;
> Those poisonous fields with rank luxuriance crowned,
> Where the dark scorpion gathers death around.
>   (ll.345–52; 4:300)

These lines have intricate relationships with other sections of the poem. The ornithological fallacy that North American songbirds had so far degenerated as to lose the power of singing is introduced to contrast with the conventional "warbling grove" and nightingales of Auburn. But the "matted woods" parallel the "tangling walks" of the now-desolate village, while the poisonous fields with their luxuriant vegetation anticipate the "potions" with which luxury destroys kingdoms (ll.385 ff.), and the "blazing suns" are as inimical as the "blazing square" (l.321) that represents the nightlife of well-to-do Londoners. As so often in Goldsmith, the poem establishes a network of contrasts and correspondences. The "solitary sports" of the new, hunting and shooting breed of landed proprietors are set against the communal festivities of the village green, while their misanthropy (spurning the cottage) stands judged by the social concern and philanthropy of the village preacher. The mingled murmur of village life is now replaced by the calls of the bittern and the lapwing, birds that love solitude and find the depopulated landscape congenial.

Most significant of the poem's contrasts is that of movement and direction. The village is deserted because, to state the obvious, everyone has deserted it. From present-day Auburn "all the bloomy flush of life is fled." "Scourged by famine" away from the "smiling land"—still fertile and beneficent, but no longer so for them—the villagers stray out to the common in hope of forage, or fly to the city for employment. The dispossessed are "called . . . away" from their native walks; with them the rural virtues and poetry itself, flying from the incursions of sensual joys, leave the land, passing from the shore on their way to unknown territories. This enforced centrifugal movement unhappily takes the place of the spontaneous congregating and circling activity that is associated with, indeed constitutes, the life of the village. Against the words "flee" and "away" are set "circle" and "around"; against the bleak "go" is the festive "go round." The tree on the village green is an important, though inanimate, pivot. The villagers "led up their sports beneath the spreading tree"; "to lead up," as of a dance, is simply to begin, but the verb also suggests a convergence upon a common meeting-point. In the tree's shade "many a pastime circled," and "sleights of art and feats of strength went round." In the village inn both news and ale circulate—the ale in fact "goes round" twice (ll.224, 248). The charms of the village shed their benign influence round its bowers, as though protectively encircling the cottages. When the church service has ended, the honest rustics gather "around the pious man," their spiritual center. The poet himself has cherished the hope of re-entering this communal existence, returning to the village of his birth and there drawing an "evening group" round his fireside. It is especially poignant, therefore, that on their last day in Auburn the emigrants tearfully "hung round" their cottages, and that when he does return the poet is forced to take "his solitary rounds"; the noun ironically evokes a sight-seeing excursion (but these are not agreeable sights), or the rounds of a watchman (but there is nothing now to watch over).

Others besides the poet are drawn in to, or back to, the village. The vagrant beggar, the cashiered soldier, the ruined spendthrift (the prodigal son returned) are all welcome in the clergyman's house. The poet's memory is activated by the places where people have gathered together, where the village has led its collective life: the church and vicarage, the schoolroom, the inn, and the green. He dwells on those activities that are conversational and convivial, on pastimes and innocent, shared mirth. The word "sports," as characterizing the life of Auburn, occurs four times in the first verse paragraph; at the beginning of the second it is those same sports that have now fled. "Rural mirth and manners are no more." Labor and piety are among the departing band of virtues (ll.397 ff.), but they are outnumbered by those qualities that bind society together: "hospitable care," "connubial tenderness," loyalty, and love.

Any deserted village is, or ought to be, a contradiction in terms, a monstrosity. Its plight naturally provokes indignation and prompts a solemn homiletic strain: "Thus fares the land, by luxury betrayed. . . ." Since the village of Auburn is additionally the poet's birthplace, to which he returns after "many a year elapsed," its ruination not only gives particular point and weight to the general protest, but also releases a different set of feelings: "Remembrance wakes with all her busy train, / Swells at my breast, and turns the past to pain" (ll.81–82). This "past" is that of the poet, rather than of the village, or of the latter only in so far as it impinged upon him. One important time span in the poem is that of the poet himself: his boyhood, the time that has gone by since he deserted his village, his concern with the close of his life, his ambition of dying at home. The poet is inevitably subject to the process of time, and his emotional involvement with Auburn leads him to project his own time scale upon it too. The drastic act of rural dispossession, presented in "The Revolution in Low Life" as a brief crisis, a dreadful turning point, becomes in the poem simultaneously a usurping, a swift replacement of one way of life by another, and a matter of gradual decay, a subjection to the passage of the years. The poem argues that in general villages are being eradicated to make living space for the rich and their retainers. If the country is the metaphorical "grave" of the rural virtues, it is also, in the eyes of the new landowners or of those who look superficially, a pleasant "garden" (l.302). But in the particular case of Auburn the cottages are left to fall into shapeless ruin, thereby providing a conventional focus for melancholy feeling. Its garden flowers run wild, its brook is now "choked with sedges," "And the long grass o'ertops the mouldering wall." The land has not been "improved" by its new proprietor, but is reverting to nature, and specifically (as I have already suggested) to the countryside familiar to Goldsmith in childhood and adolescence. The poet's nostalgia is both for the village in its happy prime, and, superimposed upon it, for the wilder reaches of the surrounding landscape, well known to him from long-distant "country excursions." So strong is this nostalgia that it disturbs and distorts what the poem claims to be saying about rural dislocation.

Memory softens and glamorizes the remembered scenes. The "contented toil" that heads the list of rural virtues is a limp cliché. Toil is something to be relaxed from. It is only in the village inn that we meet the village workforce; farmer and woodman, barber and blacksmith are there retailing news, listening to ballads, and spinning yarns. Auburn is a strongly idealized locality, charmingly without squalor or squabble, a place where the sexual relations of the young are reduced to "thefts of harmless love." The poem tends to conventionalize and simplify its pathos too. Present distresses have only the relief of tears. The widow, the sole survivor of Auburn, who scratches a meager existence among the ruins, seeks her nightly shed, and weeps till morn. The evicted villagers, unable to tear themselves away, "Returned and wept, and still returned to weep."

It is only when he invites us to consider the pitiable situation of a homeless country girl in London that Goldsmith admits the possibility that village people may be frailly human:

> Ah, turn thine eyes
> Where the poor houseless shivering female lies.
> She once, perhaps, in village plenty blest,
> Has wept at tales of innocence distressed.
> Her modest looks the cottage might adorn,
> Sweet as the primrose peeps beneath the thorn;
> Now lost to all; her friends, her virtue fled,
> Near her betrayer's door she lays her head,
> And pinched with cold, and shrinking from the shower,
> With heavy heart deplores that luckless hour,
> When idly first, ambitious of the town,
> She left her wheel and robes of country brown.
> (ll.325–26; 4:299–300)

The conduct of this young woman is not altogether intelligible. She is softhearted, and weeps the tears of sensibility, moved by stories of distress. She is modest and sweet. Yet she has not appreciated her blessings amid "village plenty," but has foolishly allowed herself to be lured away by the delights of the town, there to be seduced and abandoned by some heartless male. This misguided girl scarcely seems the sort of discontented or thoughtless person who would voluntarily ("idly") desert her village. Goldsmith, harking back to "A City Night-Piece" (the essay has many parallels with the poem) has risked implausibility in order to include a betrayed innocent in his cast of sympathetic victims.

Like the seduced village girl, Auburn is "sweet" (a frequently recurring, not to say overworked, adjective), full of "charms," the "loveliest" village of the plain. Even the mingled sounds of the village at evening behave not just like ordinary sounds but also like a bashful virgin: "These all in sweet confusion sought the shade" (l.123). "Sweet confusion" is a cliché of mid-eighteenth-century fiction, applied to sexual embarrassment. Formerly Auburn itself, or more accurately herself, was a charming, innocent maid; now she too is betrayed and abandoned. It is the village's femininity that makes it both attractive and vulnerable to predatory man. The new proprietor is a "master" who grasps the whole domain, and a "spoiler" (l.49), one who despoils the fair village:

> Sweet Auburn! parent of the blissful hour,
> Thy glades forlorn confess the tyrant's power.
> Here, as I take my solitary rounds,
> Amidst thy tangling walks, and ruined grounds. . . .
> (ll.75–78; 4:290)

"Ruined," unlike "ruinous," implies an agent of ruin, the ravager of female beauties, while "forlorn" and "tangling" suggest the distress and dishevelment of the victim of sexual aggression. The shrubs of the vicarage garden, likewise, are "torn."

The pathos of seduced females, harassed swains, and ruined bowers does not go unchecked. The poet's recollections are not without a mild amusement:

> The swain responsive as the milk-maid sung,
> The sober herd that lowed to meet their young;
> The noisy geese that gabbled o'er the pool,
> The playful children just let loose from school;

> The watch-dog's voice that bayed the whispering wind,
> And the loud laugh that spoke the vacant mind.
> (ll.117–22; 4:292)

The sounds of humanity are neatly and deflatingly paired with the sounds of animal life: "gabbled" is right both for the squawking geese and the children emerging from their schoolroom. Both schoolroom and inn provide the setting for gentle comedy: the pleasant vignette of teacher-pupil relations—"Full well they laughed, with counterfeited glee, / At all his jokes, for many a joke had he"—and the smile at rural politics: "Where village statesmen talked with looks profound, / And news much older than their ale went round." Typically sly is the comment that the schoolmaster's admired talents include an ability to "gauge," that is, to carry out measurements, but specifically to estimate the contents of barrels; he is a knowledgeable drinker. The passage that re-creates the transitory splendors of the inn parlor is fondly accurate ("nicely sanded floor"), precise in remembering the "aspen boughs, and flowers, and fennel gay" that decked the hearth in summer, and smilingly patronizing about the "broken tea-cups, wisely kept for show."

The splendor, so amiably recollected, could not "Reprieve the tottering mansion from its fall." The verb is significant; the inn is doomed by legal sentence, though also, since it belongs to the poet's past, by the sentence of time, a sentence that is more rigid and more comprehensive. If one set of female charms, those of Auburn, has been despoiled by the hand of man, those of the whole country suffer at the hand of time. The land is compared to "some fair female,"

> Secure to please while youth confirms her reign . . .
> But when those charms are past, for charms are frail,
> When time advances, and when lovers fail,
> She then shines forth, solicitous to bless,
> In all the glaring impotence of dress.
> (ll.288 ff.; 4:298)

The note of protest is blended with, and somewhat muffled by, the note of mourning for an irrecoverable past, the plangency of "no more" and "no longer" (ll.239 ff.). The poem comes close to being a "plaintive elegy." That phrase had appeared at the conclusion of the *Inquiry into Polite Learning*: "if there be a time when the muse shall seldom be heard, except in plaintive elegy, as if she wept her own decline" (1:337). At the conclusion of "The

Deserted Village," Poetry, having in effect uttered her last elegiac plaint, leaves the shores of England in the company of the rural virtues. As Auburn is, or was, the loveliest of villages, so Poetry is the "loveliest maid," timid and vulnerable. To avoid the fate of Auburn, to escape being "ruined and seduced by luxury,"[10] Poetry must flee before she too is corrupted:

> Still first to fly where sensual joys invade;
> Unfit in these degenerate times of shame
> To catch the heart, or strike for honest fame.
> Dear charming nymph, neglected and decried,
> My shame in crowds, my solitary pride.
>   (ll.408–12; 4:303)

The poet does not relish being seen to keep company with so neglected and decried a figure. But just as he begins to slide toward a maudlin self-pity ("Thou source of all my bliss and all my woe"), the real strength of this apparently frail figure is brought to mind. Poetry guides the "nobler arts" to excellence, and is the nurse of every virtue. Although she is abandoning England to its materialistic fate, her voice will not therefore be silent:

> Aid slighted truth, with thy persuasive strain
> Teach erring man to spurn the rage of gain;
> Teach him that states, of native strength possessed,
> Though very poor, may still be very blest;
> That trade's proud empire hastes to swift decay,
> As ocean sweeps the labored mole away,
> While self-dependent power can time defy,
> As rocks resist the billows and the sky.

The last four lines (the last lines of the poem) are Johnson's; his therefore are the poem's final prophetic note and its air of confidence. Plaintiveness is pushed into the background. "Can time defy" is more optimistic than "may still be very blest," and a little surprising in view of what time has been seen to accomplish in the course of the poem. Although the poet has promised, or threatened, that a land grown to "sickly greatness" through the disease of luxury must inevitably collapse (ll.389 ff.), what he has actually shown is the destruction of an agricultural community. We are now encouraged to hope that trade's proud empire really will decay, though the prophecy, as John Montague argues, has something sentimental about it, a degree of wishful thinking.[11]

With their elements of nostalgic pastoral and indignant protest, of comedy and pathos, of emotional appeal and abstract argument, "The Traveller" and "The Deserted Village" resist categorization. But since both poems are didactically passionate and socially committed, Goldsmith's friend Thomas Percy was close to the truth when he called them "his two great ethic poems."[12]

Chapter Seven
The Dramatist

Goldsmith's last and least-known play is *The Grumbler*, a one-act farce written hastily in the spring of 1773, given a single performance at the Covent Garden Theatre, and subsequently forgotten. Characteristically, it was an act of gratitude, a thank-you present for the comedian John Quick, whose performance as Tony Lumpkin had materially assisted the success of *She Stoops to Conquer* earlier that season. The farce has no claim to originality. Goldsmith made a rapid alteration of an anonymous adaption (in two acts) of Sir Charles Sedley's version (in three acts) of a five-act French comedy. But the cutting and pasting that produced this little vehicle for the virtuoso Quick were the operations of a natural dramatist. Goldsmith knew instinctively that brevity is the soul of comic writing: prolong a jest and it grows insipid. In both his major comedies scenes and encounters are kept effectively short, worked up to a comic climax and then swiftly terminated or resolved. So in *The Grumbler* he continues the process begun by his English predecessors, of condensing the French original. There is, however, one significant exception, where Goldsmith expands the text to seize a dramatic opportunity previously missed. Mr. Sourby, the grumbler, obstructs his son's marriage. To remove his objections Clarissa, his prospective daughter-in-law, pretends to be grumpy and closefisted, which ought to please the avaricious old man. In the earlier versions her assumed harshness is merely described; Sedley, for instance, has the maidservant report her mistress's severity. Goldsmith instead creates a short scene of bad temper in action, as Clarissa berates the maid.[1] It is a small but revealing demonstration of the advantage of "showing" over "telling." Goldsmith had always recognized that narration is not the dramatist's proper medium.

That Goldsmith, unlike Johnson, was by temperament a dramatist, is clear from his nondramatic writings. The introductory essay to the *Bee* dramatizes the writer's difficulties by means of a dialogue with his publisher, while in the essay on the use of language the conversation between Jack Spindle and his so-called friend is a brief and bitter exchange, complete with implied stage directions (1:354, 398). To render the noisy chaos of a club meeting, Goldsmith gives a brilliant transcript of several simultaneous dialogues and harangues, the voices cutting across one another to produce a wildly comic farrago (3:13). In *The Citizen of the World* the confrontation between Altangi and the bookseller (Letter 51) is one instance among many of a vigorously rendered dramatic scene.

Moreover, that fondness for role-playing and self-dramatization evinced in Goldsmith's youthful misadventure at the Ardagh "inn," continued throughout his life. He liked to dress up, as well as to dress finely, and was fascinated by the masquerade, with its diluted theatricality. The participants in this fashionable entertainment were all costumed, even if only in a cloak and mask, and played, even if only half-heartedly, their adopted parts of Quaker or harlequin, shepherdess or nun. In April 1772 Goldsmith was in attendance in the Pantheon rooms, wearing "old English dress," presumably the kind of doublet and hose used to represent Elizabethan dress on stage.[2] Late in 1773, in a more private frolic, he and Garrick burlesqued a speech from Addison's *Cato*. (Horace Walpole, who reported the foolery, was not amused.)[3] Less absurd and more revealing was Goldsmith's reaction to Johnson's account of his meeting with royalty. Johnson had naturally risen to the occasion: "I found his Majesty wished I should talk, and I made it my business to talk." When Johnson had concluded, Goldsmith confessed that he would have acquitted himself badly; he said this, Boswell notes, "in a kind of flutter, from imagining himself in the situation which he had just been hearing described."[4] Goldsmith was not a passive listener; he had entered into the scene.

In his earlier writings he concerned himself directly, and sometimes rashly, with theatrical affairs. He dealt shrewd blows at theater managers (*Inquiry,* chapter 12), and in a short anonymous essay of January 1760 attacked the "pantomime and monstrous farce" currently offered by the London theaters (3:54–56). His admiration for skillful and inventive comic acting, his attention to the details of stage business and eloquent gesture, which was to bear fruit in his own comedies, is already fully revealed in the *Bee* (1:360–61, 389–91).

More significantly, the seeds of his dramatic theory and practice lie in two of these early prose works. In the *Bee* for 3 November 1759 he reviews James Townley's new farce *High Life below Stairs*, in which a group of servants besport themselves while their employers are away, mimic upper-class behavior, and imbibe upper-class drinks. Goldsmith criticizes this comic device as being of limited potential: "The poor affecting the manners of the rich, might be carried on through one character or two at the most, with great propriety; but to have almost every personage on the scene almost of the same character, and reflecting the follies of each other, was unartful in the poet [i.e., author] to the last degree" (1:450). What is lacking is variety of character, variety of action (this farce is barren of incident), and originality of humor. A similar criticism could apply to a later and more varied comedy, Garrick and Colman's *The Clandestine Marriage* (1766). Here too a valet and chambermaid ape their betters by sipping chocolate and exchanging modish platitudes; the vulgar merchant Mr. Sterling imitates the gardening improvements of people of real taste; and his sister, Mrs. Heidelberg, does her best to copy fashionable behavior and pronunciation. What Goldsmith found wanting in contemporary comedy, and what he sought to provide, were comic characters who were robust and self-sufficient, with a fund of amusement inherent in the character itself, not dependent on the satirical burlesquing or inept copying of other social styles.

It follows that in his search for genuine, in every sense original, comic material, the dramatist must be willing to explore all levels of society. In eighteenth-century terms he must be willing to stoop to the "low," which means presenting humorous characters from the lower levels of society, setting scenes if necessary in such unfashionable locations as inns, and incorporating into the comic action the activities of such locations: drinking songs, irreverent behavior, rowdiness, and fisticuffs. This liberal principle of accepting humor wherever it is to be found is enunciated in a strenuously argued paragraph in the *Inquiry*:

However, by the power of one single monosyllable our critics have almost got the victory over humor amongst us. Does the poet paint the absurdities of the vulgar? Then he is *low*. Does he exaggerate the features of folly, to render it more thoroughly ridiculous? He is then very *low*. In short, they have proscribed the comic or satirical muse from every walk but high life, which though abounding in fools as well as the humblest station, is by no means so fruitful in absurdity. . . . Wit raises human nature above its [natural] level; humor acts a contrary part, and equally depresses it. To expect exalted humor is a contradiction in terms, and the critic, by demanding an impossibility from the comic poet, has in effect banished new comedies from the stage. (1:320–21)

It had not always been so. In Farquhar's *Beaux' Stratagem*, a comedy that Goldsmith admired and that plainly left its mark on *She Stoops to Conquer*, we have not only an innkeeper, on whose premises the play opens, his barmaid daughter, and a gang of shabby highwaymen, but also Squire Sullen's general factotum, the rustic and cowardly Scrub, a low but genuinely comic figure.

Tom Jones's companion Partridge has something of Scrub in his nature, and there is no shortage of inns in Fielding's first two novels. Moreover, Fielding had seized on the illogicality of decrying humor as "low" when it is in its nature to be just that. His protest and his phrasing were in Goldsmith's mind when he wrote the *Inquiry*: by their use of "the monosyllable *low*," says Fielding, the critics have succeeded in banishing all humor from the stage.[5] What the critics increasingly preferred was what came to be called "genteel comedy." By the 1750s their allegiance to this comedy of high life, a comedy too refined to admit country bumpkins or innkeepers, was so strong as to seem unshakable. Since, according to the courtesy books, it is vulgar and unbecoming to laugh heartily in public, genteel comedy is truly genteel in not evoking a loud response: low comedy "excites sudden gusts of mirth"; genteel comedy, which "speaks the language of polite life," is content with "a settled smile of pleasure."[6]

Goldsmith courageously attempted to redress the balance by introducing distinctly low characters—Timothy Twitch, bailiff, and his assistant Mr. Flanigan—into his first comedy, *The Good-Natured Man*. But gentility was not to be easily dislodged. On the opening night not only the gentlemen critics in the pit of the Covent Garden Theatre, but also the footmen, apprentices, and artisans who occupied the upper gallery, loudly and unanimously rejected the bailiff's intrusion into a bourgeois household. Whatever might occur in real life, the theater should not be thus tainted. Valets and chambermaids, who naturally belong in great houses, who are part of the decorum of polite life, can properly be seen on stage. A cockney bailiff and his Irish assistant are not decorous and should not be seen. Loud cries of "Low!" and "Damned vulgar!" rose from the pit, mingling with loud hisses from the gallery. The disturbance almost brought the play to a standstill, and the management insisted that the offending scene should be excised for the remainder of the comedy's short run. Goldsmith had to be content with its inclusion in the published text, and with defending himself in the play's preface. There he claims to be upholding an earlier comic tradition, looking back to an era when "the term *genteel comedy* was . . . unknown amongst us," and to have been inevitably led, in his pursuit of true humor, "into the recesses of the mean"; he has sought humor even "in the master of a spunging-house" (5:13–14).

Modern readers or spectators are more likely than their predecessors to feel that Goldsmith found the humor he sought. When the play enjoyed a brief revival at the National Theatre, London, in 1971, audiences clearly thought the bailiff scene was the comic high point of the action. Its comedy arises in part from Honeywood's embarrassed attempt, when the admired

Miss Richland arrives, to pass off the two sheriff's officers as naval officers. They may truthfully be said to serve the Fleet, but it is the prison of that name with which they are conversant. The subsequent, stiffly elegant conversation, about literary taste and French critics, is disastrously punctuated by the spicily colloquial and inopportune interjections of the men of law. But before Miss Richland's entrance the bailiff has been more interestingly used to expose the weakness of the good-natured man himself. We have already seen Honeywood benevolently accommodating himself to the gloom of Mr. Croaker and immediately afterward to the levity of Croaker's wife. Now it is the turn of Timothy Twitch to chime in with Honeywood's pretentious moralizing, in order to take advantage of his compliant nature. The "low" twists the genteel round its rather grubby finger:

HONEYWOOD: Tenderness is a virtue, Mr. Twitch.

BAILIFF: Ay, sir, it's a perfect treasure. I love to see a gentleman
                        with a tender heart. I don't know, but I think I have a
                        tender heart myself. If all that I have lost by my heart was
                        put together, it would make a———but no matter for that.

HONEYWOOD: Don't account it lost, Mr. Twitch. The ingratitude of the
                        world can never deprive us of the conscious happiness of
                        having acted with humanity ourselves.

BAILIFF: Humanity, sir, is a jewel. It's better than gold. I love humanity.
                        People may say that we, in our way, have no humanity.
                        But I'll show you my humanity this moment.
                        There's my follower here, little Flanigan, with a wife and
                        four children; a guinea or two would be more to him than
                        twice as much to another. Now, as I can't show him any
                        humanity myself, I must beg leave you'll do it for me.
                                                                                               (5:46)

"Humanity" is reduced to plain cash, the bailiff has baited the trap, and Honeywood obligingly opens his purse. The bailiff's response to this generous act is a perfectly judged piece of near-insolence: "Sir, you're a gentleman. I see you know what to do with your money."

Honeywood has been arrested because he imprudently stood security for a stranger. In his eyes this rash behavior is an act of exalted munificence (5:20). This young man, whose heart melts at distress whether real or fictitious, is a reworking of the Man in Black and the youthful Sir William Thornhill. Like them he does not properly value himself, as his trusty servant points out in act 1, or, as Miss Richland puts it in act 4, he has ceased to be a friend to himself. His rival in love, Mr. Lofty (a reworking of Beau Tibbs), to whom as the worthier man he is prepared to yield Miss Richland, is so blatantly unworthy, so merely a facade, that Honeywood stands condemned for sacrificing himself and, more heinously, Miss Richland. Once again Goldsmith is exposing "universal benevolence" as not only absurd in practice, as when Honeywood endeavors in alternate speeches to humor the Croakers in their diametrically opposed views (5:67–68), but also morally dangerous, an attractive screen behind which one can conceal from oneself a fundamental weakness of character, a timid desire to please and to appease. Honeywood's wishful fantasy is to be well with all the world; his fate is to be imposed on by a wheedling bailiff and a sham friend. To uphold a line of conduct, to discriminate in favor of the deserving, one needs to be able to say no. Honeywood is afraid of hostility, and incapable of taking a firm stand.

He has a good deal in common with Mr. Croaker. For Croaker, to all appearance the conventional heavy father, is really disarmingly tender. When he feels he must assume a stern tone to his "daughter" Olivia (she is in fact no relation: Goldsmith's subplot creaks most audibly), he mutters that "It goes to my heart to vex her." His assumption of an authoritarian manner is undercut by the very irony with which he seeks to strengthen it: "No, I'm to have no hand in the disposal of my own children. No, I'm nobody. I'm to be a mere article of family lumber." (5:42). This is uncomfortably near the truth, as he has already admitted to Honeywood: "you know but little of my authority at home. People think, indeed, because they see me come out in a morning thus, with a pleasant face, and to make my friends merry, that all's well within [he has just been lamenting the state of the weather, of the economy, and of the church]. But I have cares that would break an heart of stone. My wife has so encroached upon every one of my privileges, that I'm no more than a mere lodger in my own house" (5:25). Croaker's grumbling melancholy is a sort of comic stoicism, a protection against future disappointments, but also a way of claiming significance for himself. He croaks to prove that he is Mr. Croaker.

When Johnson spoke admiringly of Croaker—"there had not been of late any such character exhibited on the stage"[7]—Boswell, always quick to put Goldsmith in his place, observed that there was a clear indebtedness to Johnson's own "Suspirius," the "screech owl" of *Rambler* no. 59. (Goldsmith had already admitted the borrowing to Johnson himself.) Superficially, the obligation looks considerable. Suspirius delights in "melancholy prognosticks of the future"; Croaker has written to the newspapers on "the increase and progress of earthquakes." And Johnson notes the impact that such a negative personality makes on his acquaintance: "To those, whose weakness of spirits, or timidity of temper, subjects them to impressions from others, and who are apt to . . . catch the contagion of misery, it is extremely unhappy to live within the compass of a screech-owl's voice."[8] Mr. Honeywood has just such a "timidity of temper," and in his first scene with Croaker we see him catching "the contagion of misery" as he caps each of Croaker's dismal comments on man's dismal lot, until Croaker exclaims: "Ah, my dear friend, it is a perfect satisfaction to be miserable with you." But Suspirius is no mere complainer. He is the bitter man, embodying the discontent that each of us harbors, the irritation and envy we feel when we see others prospering. His portrait disturbs the reader, since we recognize our own malicious and denigratory impulses. That Croaker depresses those around him is true, but it is not a consequence of his malice. Some of his acquaintances attribute Dick Doleful's suicide to his having swallowed too much Croakerian conversation, but they overlook Dick's own temperament: "Poor dear Dick. He used to say that Croaker rhymed to joker, and so we used to laugh. Poor Dick"—at which Croaker pulls out his handkerchief. When Honeywood, full of sympathetic sensibility, rejoins "His fate affects me," we do not feel that he is being tempted to despair. We know his chameleon nature, and we are soon to hear Mrs. Croaker reminding him, in an echo of her husband's words, "you know I never laugh so much as with you."

The plot of *The Good-Natured Man* is designed to expose deception and prevarication. Mr. Lofty, the self-styled courtier and supposed man of affairs and influence, is finally revealed as a hollow sham. Croaker too is shown to be more softhearted than he would like to seem, while his son, Leontine, has earlier been punished for his deceptions and machinations in affairs of the heart. Between them, a teasing Miss Richland ("I must grant, sir, there are attractions in modest diffidence") and Leontine's fuming father ("silence is become his mother tongue") cover him in comic confusion (5:33–35).

The play's chief impostor is Honeywood himself, and Miss Richland is one of those who pass judgment on his dishonesty. She declares that his ridiculous discomfiture with the bailiff is "a just punishment for his dissimulation." The bailiff's arrival was itself a punitive scheme devised by Sir William Honeywood, who had taken up the financial security, to bring his nephew to his senses. In the opening scene Sir William, announcing his plot, tartly analyzes Honeywood's failings: that he indiscriminately loves all the world, and that "his good nature arises rather from his fears of offending the importunate, than his desire of making the deserving happy." In the final scene he upbraids his nephew directly and unsparingly—"Your charity, that was but injustice; your benevolence, that was but weakness"—and concludes by reproaching him for the "prostitution" of his mind. This echoes Leontine's earlier accusation that Honeywood's compliance and so-called friendship "have long been contemptible to the world," because they have been judged "as common as a prostitute's favors, and as fallacious." There is nothing genially comic about such acerbic language. Confronted by Leontine's stinging truths Honeywood can only abase himself—"I now begin to grow contemptible, even to myself. How have I sunk, by too great an assiduity to please!"—and determine on repentance in the solitude of voluntary exile (5:75–76). Forced once more, by his uncle, to look his own character in the face, he once more contemplates self-banishment; perhaps abroad he will acquire "that fortitude which may give strength to the mind, and marshal all its dissipated virtues" (5:80). But to acquire fortitude is more easily said than accomplished, as too is Sir William's final injunction: "Henceforth, nephew, learn to respect yourself." The play can end on a positive note only because Honeywood sidesteps the difficulty of growing in self-confidence and talks instead of the more accessible goal of prudent judgment, and of the educative force of love. After one last review of his by now very familiar failings, Honeywood can begin to sound cheerful: "Yes, sir, I now too plainly perceive my errors: my vanity, in attempting to please all, by fearing to offend any; my meanness, in approving folly lest fools should disapprove. Henceforth, therefore, it shall be my study to reserve my pity for real distress, my friendship for true merit, and my love for her who first taught me what it is to be happy." The play is almost ruthless in its repeated analysis and insistent exposing of its hero's folly and frailty. Its aftertaste is distinctly bitter.

She Stoops to Conquer

The preface to *The Good-Natured Man* asserts that French comedy has already become "very elevated and sentimental," and hopes that false refinement will not have the same effect in the British theater, of banishing humor and character. The dedication of *She Stoops to Conquer* (1773) accepts the reality that sentimental comedy has now crossed the Channel and established itself as the reigning fashion. In thanking Johnson for his moral support, Goldsmith affirms, a little boastfully, that to have attempted a comedy that was "not merely sentimental" was a very dangerous undertaking, in effect another of his considerable risks. In swimming against the fashionable tide he faced a real possibility of financial failure and literary humiliation. The manager of the Covent Garden Theatre made no secret of his lack of faith in the play; three members of the company went further, and withdrew their services. The author's own nervousness is suggested by the writing of "An Essay on the Theatre," anonymously published in the *Westminster Magazine* some ten weeks before the play opened. The essay attempts to dislodge, by argument and ridicule, a comic mode that is admitted to be modish, and to gain a fair hearing for a more traditional, a purer kind of comedy. "Which deserves the preference: the weeping sentimental comedy, so much in fashion at present, or the laughing and even low comedy, which seems to have been last exhibited by Vanbrugh and Cibber?" (3:210). Goldsmith presumably alludes to *The Provoked Husband; or, A Journey to London*, the comedy begun by Vanbrugh, completed by Cibber, and favorably received at Drury Lane in 1728. Its low (and effective) comedy is confined to the subplot, in which a provincial family bumbles about the metropolis. Its main plot, however, is unmistakably genteel, not to say aristocratic, in tone, and the anguish and complications are resolved in a tearful scene of reconciliation. These are moral tears, as the heroine renounces a life of gambling and dissipation. What Goldsmith condemns, when he speaks of "weeping sentimental comedy," is the vogue for tears of a simply pathetic kind, the tears of distressed innocence, and what seemed to him to have turned a growing tendency into an overwhelming tide, was the advent of Richard Cumberland. His first three important and popular comedies, *The Brothers*, *The West Indian*, and *The Fashionable Lover*, appeared in the five years between *The Good-Natured Man* and *She Stoops to Conquer*. By the beginning of 1773 Goldsmith believed that a new "species of bastard tragedy," exemplified by Cumberland, had driven robust, laughing comedy from the stage. So he argues in his essay that comedy forsakes its traditional and proper role if, instead of attending to vices and follies, it depicts the amiable virtues of private life: loyalty, affability, sincerity, and so on. The audience is invited not to sit in moral judgment (though to be fair to Cumberland, some of his minor characters are held up to comic ridicule), but to bathe in warm, outgoing, even ecstatic emotions, to feel with Belcour, the hero of *The West Indian*, as he cries "O bliss unutterable!" We are asked to endorse the dramatist's claim that the good heart of a Belcour or a Lord Ogleby (finally generous in *The Clandestine Marriage*) will excuse their earlier foibles, and we do so the more readily because this flatteringly proves us to be tenderhearted and forgiving. We leave the theater in a glow of satisfaction and self-applause.

Sentimental comedy has a further advantage: it is easy to write. Goldsmith's essay offers a recipe for instant success. Take a genteel hero and heroine, perhaps endowed with aristocratic titles, "put an insipid dialogue, without character or humor, into their mouths, give them mighty good hearts . . . [and] make a pathetic scene or two, with a sprinkling of tender melancholy conversation through the whole."[9] The "pathetic scene" and "melancholy conversation" are sentimental in a sense we still recognize: plangent, emotionally distressful, seeking the pity and even the tears of the spectators. The speeches in such a comedy will also be "sentimental" in a more restricted, peculiarly eighteenth-century sense: full of finely tuned sensibility, expressing a scrupulous, high-minded delicacy of feeling. More specifically, these speeches will be stuffed with fine "sentiments," laudable principles firmly enunciated by characters of approved moral worth, who preface their wisdom with easily recognized signals ("It is my maxim that . . . "; "I was going to observe . . ."), and who enjoy exchanging platitudes with ladies and gentlemen of similar dispositions.

In this last sense Honeywood is a man of sentiment: "It is my maxim, sir, that crimes generally punish themselves" (5:68). So, to our surprise, are Dick Muggins the exciseman, and the bear-leader, two of Tony Lumpkins's tavern companions. Tony's associates have already been written off by his mother as "a low, paltry set of fellows." The jest, which Goldsmith borrows from Fielding, is to make these low individuals, in the low milieu of the Three Pigeons, misuse the current cant of gentility to repudiate the low in art.[10] The horse-doctor approves of Tony's choice of song: "he never gives us nothing that's *low*." And Dick Muggins opines: "The genteel thing is the genteel thing at any time—if so be that a gentleman bees in a concatenation ackoardingly"—a mysterious piece of wisdom, but couched in fashionable terminology ("concatenation" was a vogue word). It elicits a matching response from his companion, the bear-leader: "I like the maxum of it, Master Muggins." Here both word and pronunciation are sentimentally correct; in *The Clandestine Marriage* Mrs. Heidelberg affects "maxum" as the language of "qualaty," while even Timothy Twitch has picked it up, perhaps from having arrested his social superiors (5:46). Gentility, as the bear-leader argues, may not be such an exclusive thing after all: "What though I am obligated to dance a bear? A man may be a gentleman for all that." Even a gentleman may have to earn his living, and the bear in question dances only to "the very genteelest of tunes," melodies from the operas (most expensive and therefore most fashionable of entertainments) of Arne and Handel.

The master of fine sentiments in *She Stoops to Conquer* is its hero, Charles Marlow; at least he would be so, were he master of his nerves. His problem is that while he can be sprightly enough with a barmaid, he is horribly tongue-tied in the presence of what he calls a "modest woman," one who is too decorous to flirt. Unexpectedly confronted by Miss Kate Hardcastle, a

young lady of modesty and reputation, selected by his father as an eligible
match, Marlow is so abashed that he is literally unable to look her in the
face—an inability on which the plot heavily depends. Goldsmith keeps him
at a formal, embarrassed distance from her, and in the ensuing dialogue
mocks the frigid discourses of sentiment. Since bland commonplace is the
stuff of such discourse, one speaker can easily assist another. Marlow endeavors to propound some unexceptionable sentiments: "In this age of hypocrisy there are few who, upon strict inquiry, do not—a — a — a —."
Kate, perceiving his sententious drift better than he does, can rescue him
without much intellectual effort: "You mean, that in this hypocritical age
there are few that do not condemn in public what they practice in private."
Marlow thankfully accepts this exemplary wisdom, and in proper sentimental vein caps one truism with another: "Those who have most virtue in their
mouths, have least of it in their bosoms." Goldsmith thus neatly illustrates
the tendency of sentimental dialogue; it does not simply stagnate, but goes
round in ever-decreasing circles. Kate, who has begun the encounter by pretending to delight in grave conversation, and to approve a "man of *sentiment*," ends by laughingly inquiring of the audience (Marlow has extricated
himself from the conversation and the room), "Was there ever such a sober,
sentimental interview?"

Their later interviews, when Kate stoops to conquer by assuming, first,
the manner of a barmaid, then that of a poor relation of the Hardcastles,
are decidedly more spirited. She is too energetic and confident to be af-
flicted with sentimental distress; the tears she sheds in act 4 are a pretense,
and therefore a satire on sentiment, a ruse for which Marlow instantly and
comically falls: "By heaven, she weeps. This is the first mark of tenderness
I ever had from a modest woman, and it touches me." Genuine distress is
confined to the subplot, when at the end of the same act Mrs. Hardcastle
successfully obstructs the elopement of her ward Constance Neville and
Marlow's friend Hastings. "Disappointment" and "distress" are invoked
by the frustrated lovers, but are countered both by Marlow's recriminations and by the presence of Tony Lumpkin. He is the surly butt of the
lovers' rage, since it is his illiteracy that has given the elopement plot away;
he is also their cunning savior. Even as the act ends he is contriving a stratagem to set all to rights.

The main plot is not without some of the trappings of genteel
eighteenth-century comedy: the hero's father is Sir Charles Marlow, as
Honeywood's uncle is Sir William Honeywood, knight of the Bath. In the
subplot conventional features are quite pronounced. Constance is the vulnerable orphan, under strong pressure to give her hand in marriage to Tony.

Her lover's language is stereotyped: his "Let us fly, my charmer" is met by Constance's prudent sententiousness: "In the moment of passion, fortune may be despised, but it ever produces a lasting repentance." A performance that verged on the burlesque at moments like these would not be out of keeping with the spirit of the play, nor with Mrs. Hardcastle's sneer when the lovers finally appeal to her husband's humanity and there is much talk of justice, duty, and tenderness: "Pshaw, pshaw, this is all but the whining end of a modern novel." In fact the resolution of difficulties is achieved not by the author's romantic wand but by the rather squalid, certainly ungenteel, revelation that Mrs. Hardcastle has deceived her son about his age. He is, unbeknown to himself, more than 21 years old and free to refuse Constance, which he forthrightly does. In *The Good-Natured Man* all is reconciled in the low surroundings of an inn, the setting for the final act; here the habitué of the Three Pigeons removes the last obstacle in the way of happiness for the earnest Constance and Hastings.

After many setbacks the representative of "fun" is triumphant in the subplot. As for the main plot, that same figure is its begetter; a comic action that ends with the exposing of a mercenary lie about Tony, has begun with Tony's own, ultimately beneficent falsehood. From his initial prank, and Marlow's mistaken belief that Hardcastle's home is the Buck's Head Inn, comes the union of the lovers. Once Tony has put his plan into effect, his stepsister Kate can shrewdly take advantage of the situation. The two of them have mischievousness in common, and each is most imperceptively described by a fond parent as "pretty innocence" (5:111, 188). The play's structure, however, carefully keeps them apart (only in the final scene are they on stage together), so that their schemings can run on separate tracks. Kate overcomes the obstacles that Marlow's personality puts across her route to marriage; Tony, with variable success, tackles the external difficulties, especially that posed by Mrs. Hardcastle, that beset the path to matrimony of Constance and Hastings. The progress of the subplot, dominated by Tony's animal spirits, appropriately depends on, or is thwarted by, physical objects and physical acts: the box of jewels; the letter that Hastings writes to arrange transport for the elopement; the climactic coach ride round and round the Hardcastle estate, which ends up in the discomfort of the horsepond.

Whereas Kate is a skillful actress, her stratagem proceeding smoothly toward its target, in the subplot ingenuity continually defeats itself, or is summarily punished, or produces quite unlooked-for consequences. The jewel box, stolen by Tony, is returned to his mother's safekeeping by Marlow, who takes her to be the landlady; Tony's overarching hoax on the travelers baffles his subordinate project. The contents of Hastings's letter come to light because Constance is just too clever in inventing a communication about cockfighting. As Tony ruefully admits, "I thought you could never be making believe." Earlier he has deliberately misinterpreted his mother's real consternation over the jewels—"how she fidgets and spits about like a catherine-wheel"—as brilliant make-believe: "I never saw it better acted in my life." Exasperated, she sets about him, but not before she has betrayed, in the stress of the moment, an uncharacteristic compassion for Miss Neville: "My poor niece, what will become of her?" There is a similar unexpected gush of real feeling, and similarly in the midst of a farcical situation, when Tony's final trick, the circular coach ride, is brought to nothing. His improvised fiction, that Mr. Hardcastle, enjoying an evening stroll in his garden, is a dangerous highwayman, is frustrated as his mother comes from her hiding place and kneels before her husband: "Here, good gentleman, whet your rage upon me. Take my money, my life, but spare that young gentleman, spare my child." So Goldsmith continues to play with the concept of gentility. A villainous "fellow" (Tony's dismissive term for the "highwayman") becomes a "good gentleman" when he threatens one's life; and the life of a "young gentleman" is a life worth saving, though only Mrs. Hardcastle, and she only in an emergency, would so label the graceless varlet her son. In fairness to her, she has tried to qualify him for the role; she once embroidered a waistcoat for him, to make him genteel (5:153).

As she vainly tries to convince Tony that the jewels really are stolen, Mrs. Hardcastle desperately protests: "Was there ever such a blockhead, that can't tell the difference between jest and earnest?" (5:166). Her question could stand as the epigraph for the subplot. The principal action is fairly summed up in Marlow's not dissimilar admission: "My stupidity saw everything the wrong way" (5:185). But his failure to see clearly and straight (by a nice irony he is made to pretend to think that Kate squints [5:170, 172]), and his persistence in mistaking Hardcastle's house for an inn, have unsettling results, not merely for himself but also for the proprietor. As Marlow takes his impudent liberties he turns Hardcastle's world upside down. He encourages his servants to get drunk, quite the gentlemanly thing to do, since the publican will not be the loser. He thus unwittingly brings the low atmosphere of the Three Pigeons up the hill and into the residence of "one of the best families in the county." Hardcastle's private house becomes a public house, and when a drunken servant is summoned to prove his master's magnanimousness, Hardcastle's patience snaps. "I say this house is mine, sir; this house is mine, and I command you to leave it directly." In response Marlow merely laughs, as at a landlord behaving absurdly out of character: "Ha! ha! ha! A puddle in a storm. I shan't stir a step, I assure you. (*In a serious tone*) This, your house, fellow? [With "fellow" he brutally propels Hardcastle down several rungs of the social ladder.] It's my house. This is my house, mine while I choose to stay. What right have you to bid me leave this house, sir? I never met with such impudence, curse me, never in my whole life before" (5:182). The barrage of personal pronouns gives great force to this assault on the sacred notion of property. If a man cannot call his house his own—and Hardcastle's name suggests the proverbial dogma that a man's home is his castle—then what is eighteenth-century society coming to? For a perilous moment the comedy threatens disorder and anarchy, a feast of misrule. But not subversiveness or political radicalism. It is Marlow's mis-seeing that is to blame. Once his vision is corrected, social norms and proprieties are reestablished, and property is restored to its rightful owner; Marlow duly prepares to leave. That Goldsmith, for all the seriousness of his moral protest, is content to treat disruptive social protest as matter for jest, has been revealed earlier in the scene. Marlow's servant utters stirring democratic words—"Though I'm but a servant, I'm as good as another man"—but he utters them in his cups, and his egalitarianism is compromised by his drunkenness. Similarly, the anonymous threatening letter, a crude but serious expression of agrarian discontent in the second half of the eighteenth century, is for Goldsmith material only for comedy. The specimen in *The Citizen of the World* is laughable by reason of its zany illogicality (2:416–17), and that in *The Good-Natured Man* because of its imperfect grasp of orthography—"the genuine incendiary spelling" (5:62).

Tony is not present to witness the puzzlement and perturbation of his stepfather in this scene of confrontation, and cannot relish the full consequences of his initial trick. For that trick was devised not only to humble the two supercilious London gentlemen, but also so that Tony could be "revenged upon the old grumbletonian" who continually calls his stepson whelp and hound (5:119). Even as he contemplates revenge, however, Tony checks himself: "But then, I'm afraid." He may confidently rule the roost at the Three Pigeons, as the late Squire Lumpkin's son, but at home, though mischievous he is also compliant, even sulkily abject. His character and conduct have more in common with Marlow's than we may at first suspect. Both have to be humored like spoiled children. Neither can bear to be disappointed, Tony of his alehouse fun, Marlow of his comforts on the road. And Marlow is certainly fearful. He dreads the terrors of a formal courtship, and talks of running the gauntlet of the whole of the landlord's family. His "unaccountable reserve" (Hasting's phrase) even prevents him from asking directions from strangers. "I am," he confesses, "unwilling to lay myself under an obligation to everyone I meet, and often stand the chance of an unmannerly answer" (5:119). Being afraid of a hostile response, of rudeness, he exaggerates the peril ("everyone," "often"); lacking confidence in handling even a casual social encounter, he sees it in terms of an obligation imposed on him, and therefore something that he can reasonably avoid.

Marlow can be himself only when those he encounters have clearly defined social roles (unlike strangers accidentally met) and clearly defined relationships with himself. Since his life so far has been "chiefly spent in a college or an inn," the roles so far have been restricted in number. A landlord is, or ought to be, complaisant and unobtrusive. Barmaids and college bedmakers can be expected to be forward and flirtatious with a young gentleman, without any serious consequences on his side. The status of these people is unambiguous: a landlord is a "fellow," and servingwomen are "females of another class" than modest women. With such people he enjoys the freedom to release the wilder, more aggressive side of his personality, what the play calls his "impudence." It is clearly manifested in his discourteous treatment of Hardcastle's conversational gambits and bill of fare, and in his "hauling about" and attempting to kiss the apparent barmaid of the Buck's Head. Marlow claims that female domestics, milliners' apprentices, and the like "are of *us*," not a race apart, but ready to reciprocate the man's advances because they share something of his sexual freedom and irresponsibility, and are willing to enter into the spirit of his game. When a barmaid says "no," she is not being rude and unmannerly, for she actually means "yes." So the women are "of *us*" because they can be relied on to satisfy a gentleman's appetites, without laying him under an obligation; in no sense are they worthy of his esteem. When Marlow gloats over the "tempting, brisk, lovely little thing that runs about the house with a bunch of keys at its girdle," he is mildly reproved by his friend: "how can *you*, Charles, go about to rob a woman of her honor?" The reply is revealing: "Pshaw, pshaw, we all know the honor of the barmaid of an inn. I don't intend to *rob* her . . . there's nothing in this house I shan't honestly *pay* for" (5:177–78). The italics are Goldsmith's. Transactions in inns, whether with landlords or barmaids, are satisfactorily commercial; the only obligations are financial, and soon removed. Appropriately, Marlow tells the "barmaid" that his name is Mr. Solomons, hinting that he is a Jewish moneylender. But if they are commercial, the dealings are not simply neutral and unemotional. Marlow has already announced: "I'm doomed to adore the sex, and yet to converse with the only part of it I despise."

Since Marlow feels secure only with those he looks down on, since he fears rejection, then to recognize that he is in fact contemptible is, as it was for Honeywood, cataclysmic. When he discovers that he has been duped by Tony and kept in the dark by Hastings, he bitterly reproaches them: "So, I have been finely used here among you—rendered contemptible, driven into ill manners [a neat evasion of his own responsibility], despised, insulted, laughed at" (5:192). The verbs are carefully ordered, building to a climax. Significantly, his one moment of doubt about the "barmaid" occurs when he suspects that she is laughing at him, something that real barmaids do not do (5:173). That briefly gives him pause. At the end, when all his mistakes are revealed, Kate's relentless teasing is a fate that is "worse than death" (5:212). What he most dreads has come about: he is a laughingstock. Like Honeywood once again, he is ready to run away to hide his shame. He is detained by Hardcastle, who with the brief injunction "Take courage, man" hands him over to Kate for his final testing. According to the stage direction the couple retire to the back-scene, "she tormenting him." The dumbshow continues while the subplot is sorted out. Finally Kate, without speaking another word, allows her hand to be joined to his.

By suppressing their dialogue of reconciliation Goldsmith slides over the problem of having Marlow openly avow and excuse his silly dissimulation as Mr. Solomons, alias the "agreeable Rattle" of the Ladies' Club in London. By clearing up the mistake about the inn well before that concerning Kate's identity, Goldsmith has already led us to think that if barmaids are not in question the man may be honorable after all. Kate proves this by deftly moving into her second role: the house is no inn, and the girl he took for a barmaid is actually a poor relation of the family, a dependent who acts as housekeeper. She can now seem priggishly virtuous, shocked at the idea of being wrongly identified: "Dear me! Dear me! I'm sure there's nothing in my *behavior* [being a poor relation she is a trifle undereducated] to put me upon a level with one of that stamp" (5:185). She thus cunningly leads Marlow to believe that it is his vision that has been faulty, not her conduct that has been modified. As he readily admits, "I mistook your assiduity for assurance, and your simplicity for allurement." She had indeed shown assurance and allurement in her barmaid role, but men who are falling in love can adjust their mental focus with great rapidity. The change in her status is not immediately sufficient to allow a conventional and timid young man to think of marriage: "the difference of our birth, fortune, and education, make an honorable connection impossible"; "were I to live for myself alone, I could easily fix my choice; but I owe too much to the opinion of the world, too much to the authority of a father." But combined with her sham tears the rise in status is just enough to make him behave in a more principled manner: "I can never harbor a thought of seducing simplicity that trusted in my honor, or bringing ruin upon one whose only fault was being too lovely." To this declaration Kate responds, in an aside, "Generous man! I now begin to admire him." Such overvaluing of his conduct suggests that Kate's mental focus is undergoing rapid adjustment too.

Kate's is a superb role for a virtuoso comic actress. As barmaid she is neatly disingenuous about the nectar that Marlow would like to taste on her lips ("that's a liquor there's no call for in these parts—French, I suppose"), and arch in her reaction to his compliments: "O la, sir, you'll make one ashamed." As poor relation she is straightforward, sincere, a little on her dignity, and naively repetitive ("I'm sure" occurs five times in three speeches). Her vivacity and enterprise, the delight she takes in her impersonations, together with the complete success of her stratagem, may obscure the fact that while the play seems to accord her a large degree of independence, it traps her in a realm of male fantasy. She is the ideal woman for a great many men, because through her different identities she proves herself all things to one man: the Miss Hardcastle who is well-bred, well-dressed, and well-to-do, an excellent match; the vivacious coquette who is pertly flirtatious and sexually exciting; the poor relation who is modest, simple, undemanding, true, generous-hearted. If she is trapped in a world of masculine values she is a complicit prisoner, since in stooping to conquer she is willing to descend from her station in life to satisfy Marlow's inclinations, willing to become the sexual plaything that he enjoys yet despises. Her father, thoroughly masculine, thinks that she has satisfied her own inclinations too, since "girls like to be played with, and rumpled a little too, sometimes" (5:198).

The play's title, perhaps unwisely, forces the idea of social descent on our attention. An alternative, "The Belle's Stratagem," proposed by Reynolds, would have played down Kate's demeaning of herself and would have pointed up the relationship with Farquhar. Both titles give prominence to the heroine's initiative, whereas the play's concern is with the hero's infirmity of temper, his comic blunders and confusions, and the correcting of his vision. What Kate's therapy effects is a moderating of his "impudence" and a hardening of his "modesty" (the two keywords threaten at times to become obtrusive, perhaps more so in the theater than in the study). The shocking effrontery that he shows on first meeting Mr. Hardcastle, and the disabling shyness that he displays on first meeting his daughter, move toward a common ground of confidence and commitment as he declares his true feelings and makes his proposal of marriage (still ignorant of Kate's identity): "I can have no happiness but what's in your power to grant me" (5:211).

Throughout the later part of this crucial, final interview between the lovers, their fathers are concealed listeners. Their bewildered reactions ensure that the most serious moment of the play does not lapse into solemnity. The healing of the division in Marlow's nature is achieved by essentially comic means: Kate's amusing and amused playacting, and, to begin with, Tony's hoax. Goldsmith was always fascinated by practical jokes. Alexis Pyron's *La Métromanie* (Verse-mania), which he calls "infinitely the best modern performance upon the French theater" (3:246), is founded on a hoax that its author had played on Voltaire. And the action of *The Good-Natured Man* develops from Sir William's grim device of having his nephew arrested. But in neither play does the joke produce both such hilarious repercussions and such romantic and wholesome effects. Evidently, as the action of *She Stoops to Conquer* proves, to banish comedy in favor of sentiment would be to banish a genuinely benevolent spirit, something that makes for happiness.

The play also demonstrates that to banish laughter is, fortunately, an impossibility. When, at the opening of act 2, Hardcastle is drilling his servants, he instructs them how to behave, and therefore how to preserve social boundaries, if he should happen to tell a good story while they are waiting at table: "you must not all burst out a-laughing, as if you made part of the company." Laughter, however, ignores social distinctions, as Diggory points out: "Then ecod your worship must not tell the story of Ould Grouse in the gun-room. I can't help laughing at that—he ! he ! he !—for the soul of me. We have laughed at that these twenty years." He bursts into merriment at the mere recollection, and Hardcastle joins him, before graciously approving: "Well, honest Diggory, you may laugh at that." In the theater we may ourselves smile condescendingly at Hardcastle's absurd granting of permission, and we may smile appreciatively at the idea that comedy can break down social barriers. But we shall undoubtedly find ourselves laughing aloud while Hardcastle, Diggory, and the other servants are enjoying their joke. We laugh at their laughter—we can laugh at nothing else, because the story of Old Grouse remains a complete mystery. What did the gun-dog get up to in the gun-room? We may safely conjecture that the story would have been a "low" one. We can certainly acknowledge that to make an audience laugh over a nonexistent joke is one of the play's oddest triumphs. If laughter is thus self-generating it will be very difficult to get rid of.

Epilogue

Late in 1773 Goldsmith wrote to Garrick that in a season or two he would have another comedy ready for the stage, a promise Garrick dismissed as so much idle talk: he endorsed the letter "Goldsmith's Parlaver."[1] We shall never know how firm Goldsmith's intentions were. Two months later he was suffering from kidney disease, the consequence of a bladder infection that had manifested itself intermittently during the past two years. By the end of March he was gravely ill, feverish and unable to eat. He died early on the morning of Monday, 4 April 1774.

His posthumously published works show that some of his projects reached full growth. Largest in scale is the eight-volume *History of the Earth and Animated Nature*, much of it systematically compiled from standard scientific sources, but with sudden disarming abandonments of scientific method—"I call a squirrel an animal of the hare kind, because it is something like a hare"[2]—and with appeals to personal experience that unexpectedly make this textbook one of the most autobiographically revealing of his works. He has, he tells us, seen "a kind of floating bee-house" in France and Piedmont; as a child he has, like other country children, hunted and destroyed bees to get at their honey-bags. He has pursued dragonflies, wandered in the sedgy moors where lapwings breed, and noted, "in the place where I was a boy," the superstitious terror struck through a whole village by the boom of a bittern. The droll account of the nesting habits of rooks uses his own observations from his window in the Temple, the home and headquarters of lawyers, and with amusing appropriateness talks of the "legal constitution" of a rookery, and the complaints brought against, and punishments inflicted on, those thieving birds that take shortcuts in nest building.

At times more serious preoccupations invigorate Goldsmith's prose. In his account of the partridge he deprecates the game laws, which are designed to ensure that "the poor shall abstain from what the rich have taken a fancy to keep for themselves." And he opens his chapter on the cow with a reminder of its economic significance. It is "the poor man's pride, his riches, and his support. There are many of our peasantry that have no other possession but a cow." The poor, however, must sell the milk and butter it produces to their masters, so as to provide their own more meager fare. They must fatten the calf for market, "since veal is a delicacy they could not make any pretensions to." So they are only the "nominal possessors" of their live-stock, a situation that moves Goldsmith to passionate protest: "I cannot bear to hear the rich crying out for liberty, while they thus starve their fellow-creatures, and feed them up with an imaginary good, while they monopolize the real benefits of nature." Goldsmith speaks of "our peas-antry," implying that of Britain in general. It is probable that he is thinking particularly of conditions in Ireland.[3]

Even in *The Grecian History* (published 15 June 1774), a work for the most part flatly competent, Goldsmith's political and social concerns can be glimpsed. The progression of the narrative enforces the historical argument against luxury: the Greeks gradually forsake the paths of hardy virtue for a life of opulence and enervation. We are reminded that the Spartan senate was deliberately instituted to "serve as a counterpoise" to the prerogatives of the king on one side, and the demands of the people on the other. But the moment in Greek history that rouses Goldsmith's imagination is the Athe-nians' departure from their city in the face of the Persian invader: "A brave, generous, polite, and ancient people, now forced from their native seats to undergo all the vicissitudes and dangers of the sea." The idea of enforced de-parture produces yet another "formal tableau of pathos,"[4] as Goldsmith de-tails the fond affection of the women for their homes, the steadiness and courage of some of the Athenians, the "pious resignation" of all.[5]

By an irony Goldsmith would no doubt have appreciated, these two sub-stantial works are now largely unread, while two pieces of verse that were al-most certainly never designed for publication are invariably taken into account in any assessment of his poetical skills. "The Haunch of Venison" (published 1776) is Goldsmith's lighthearted version of the uncomfortable dinner party, a satirical set piece found in Horace and Juvenal, Boileau and Rochester, Pope and Smollett. Like his predecessors Goldsmith mocks him-self: "So next day in due splendor to make my approach, / I drove to his door in my own hackney coach"—a poor author has to rely on public trans-port. His discomfiture at table is a direct consequence of his own social pre-tensions. He has bragged, in the manner of Beau Tibbs and Mr. Lofty, that his haunch of venison is not such an uncommon gift for him to receive: "Some lords, my acquaintance, that settle the nation, / Are pleased to be kind—but I hate ostentation." He suffers accordingly, amongst vulgar, greedy company, and endures the final disappointment of the nonappear-ance of the venison pasty at this wretched meal. The poem makes comic capital out of disaster, even pretending to laugh at itself. It is no "Poetical Epistle," as it proclaims itself to be, but a private, entertaining, gossipy let-

ter in verse. Yet it reminded its recipient, Lord Clare, and now informs a
wider readership, that among his numerous and varied acquaintances Goldsmith could count a noble lord. The satire on the "underbred" host and his
low habitat gains its force both from the dramatic portrayal of crude ill
manners, and from the implicit contrast with aristocratic standards of generosity ("Thanks, my lord, for your venison . . .") and modest good taste.

"The Haunch of Venison" was written during the winter of 1770–71.
Goldsmith's last, unfinished, verse composition was "Retaliation," a poem
in the same anapestic couplet form. Its origins lie in the regular gatherings
of a group of friends at the St. James's Coffee House. On one occasion,
probably in January 1774, members of the group set themselves to write
extempore epitaphs on one another, or (in a different version of the events)
Garrick and Goldsmith challenged one another to this poetic duel. Garrick
was first to strike: "Here lies Nolly Goldsmith, for shortness called Noll, /
Who wrote like an angel, but talked like poor Poll." Goldsmith retired to
consider how to revenge himself, how to do himself justice, and how he
might deal justly with Garrick and the rest. As he had written in an early
letter, retaliation is "the most equitable law in nature."[6] It is fitting that his
final work should have been an act of justice, since he had always prized fair
play. The result of his cogitations is a sequence of epitaphs, in alphabetical
order from Barnard to Reynolds (that on John Ridge was never written), introduced by a gathering more amiable than that in "The Haunch of Venison," but leading to greater disarray:

> Here waiter, more wine! Let me sit while I'm able,
> Till all my companions sink under the table;
> Then with chaos and blunders encircling my head,
> Let me ponder, and tell what I think of the dead.
>   (ll.19–22; 4:353)

Goldsmith's manner is zestful and high-spirited as he confronts the varied
phenomena of his friends' personalities. There is the enigmatic William
Burke, the pupil of impulse, "His conduct still right, with his argument
wrong," and that provoking devil Richard Burke, whose frolics were at the
same time irritating and agreeable, and whose epitaph is most unsolemnly
frolicsome, with a jokey rhyme ("sigh at"/"quiet") and playful zeugma:
"Now breaking a jest, and now breaking a limb." Goldsmith takes full advantage of the principle of variation within a single formal category that he
had employed to such effect in the letters of *The Citizen of the World*. The
portrait of Reynolds is free of all qualification—"He has not left a better or

wiser behind"—though it permits a smile at Reynolds pretending to be more deaf than he really was when in the company of pseudoconnoisseurs. That of Dr. John Douglas, arch-exposer of literary frauds, allows the poet to be self-deprecatory: he will now be able to compile his books without fear that his plagiarism or ignorance will be detected. The first epitaph, on Dr. Thomas Barnard, ends a little tartly, with the poet reporting the gossip of Barnard's detractors—an epitaph may after all be the better for being impartial; that on Joseph Hickey ends somewhat pointedly too, revealing the man's profession as "a special attorney": this, it turns out, is the "fault" in his character that the poet has teasingly invited the reader to guess.

While the lines on Hickey are rhythmically complex, enacting the give and take of dialogue, those on Edmund Burke deliberately rock back and forth to express the paradoxical verdict that Goldsmith is compelled to bring in—"Though equal to all things, for all things unfit"—and the poles of Burke's nature that (such are the times) unfit him for the proper and profitable use of his manifold talents: "Too nice for a statesman, too proud for a wit, / For a patriot too cool, for a drudge disobedient, / And too fond of the *right* to pursue the *expedient*." His very virtues mean that he cannot be accommodated in the shabbily selfish world of eighteenth-century politics. Should he have entered that world in the first place?

Naturally, given the poem's genesis, the longest epitaph is Garrick's (ll.93–124), an act of retaliation that throws back with equal wit the jibe about Goldsmith's shortness ("An abridgement of all that was pleasant in man"), and with quiet malice recalls Garrick's tribute that Goldsmith "wrote like an angel": "But peace to his spirit, wherever it flies, / To act as an angel, and mix with the skies." The man's shortcomings, and the basic contradiction in his nature, are put before us in a half-apologetic manner that damns with understatement: "On the stage he was natural, simple, affecting, / 'Twas only that, when he was off, he was acting." So he will, in his immortal form, continue to act, which is not quite what one expects of an angel. There is in this epitaph no lack of compliments, but no lack of outspoken criticism either:

> As an actor, confessed without rival to shine,
> As a wit, if not first, in the very first line;
> Yet with talents like these, and an excellent heart,
> The man had his failings, a dupe to his art.
> Like an ill-judging beauty his colors he spread,
> And beplastered with rouge his own natural red.

There is something frenetic about Garrick, a need to be active, so that he must be continually and perversely angling for his friends' affections, though he knows that those affections are securely his. This, for someone like Goldsmith who values sincerity in personal relations, is bad enough. But Garrick's greatest failing is his inordinate love of praise, which thus gives Goldsmith his last opportunity to state a recurrent theme. Since he is a glutton for praise, Garrick's taste becomes vitiated, demanding ever more fulsome adulation: "Who peppered the highest was surest to please." The trade between the flattered and his toadies belittles both parties:

> If dunces applauded he paid them in kind.
> Ye Kenricks, ye Kellys, and Woodfalls so grave,
> What a commerce was yours, while you got and you gave!
> How did Grubstreet reecho the shouts that you raised,
> While he was berosciused, and you were bepraised.

The portrait of the dramatist Richard Cumberland (ll.61–78) is the most finely judged of all, astutely balanced between praise and blame. If Goldsmith was stepping cautiously because of Cumberland's well-known irascibility, he succeeded perfectly: Cumberland expressed his grateful delight at the lines. Robert Hopkins, reading between them, finds that Cumberland is covertly being attacked for hypocrisy and egotism.[7] Goldsmith plainly disapproves of Cumberland's comic practice, as he had already made clear in the "Essay on the Theatre":

> His gallants are all faultless, his women divine,
> And comedy wonders at being so fine. . . .
> His fools have their follies so lost in a crowd
> Of virtues and feelings, that folly grows proud,
> And coxcombs, alike in their failings alone,
> Adopting his portraits, are pleased with their own.

To conceive of comedy's role as flattering rather than critical, is a kind of sickness, though Goldsmith softens the charge by implying that it does not originate with Cumberland:

> Say, where has our poet this malady caught,
> Or wherefore his characters thus without fault?
> Say, was it that vainly directing his view

> To find out men's virtues, and finding them few,
> Quite sick of pursuing each troublesome elf,
> He grew lazy at last, and drew from himself?

Cumberland's idea of comedy is faulty, but the virtues of his amiable characters turn out, charmingly, to be his own. This is a kind of raillery that does not wholly subsume its initial criticism in its final compliment.

In one of his earliest contributions to the *Monthly Review* Goldsmith had praised Mr. Connoisseur, the author of the periodical of that name, for being "perfectly satirical, yet perfectly good-natured" (1:14). In the epitaph on Cumberland, but in earlier writings too, he could claim to have followed the *Connoisseur*'s difficult lead. That the ideal was still before him is suggested by his self-description at the beginning of "Retaliation," where the dinner guests are designated in terms of dishes of food. The eloquent Burke is "tongue, with a garnish of brains"; the caustic Ridge is anchovy, the gentle Reynolds lamb. Goldsmith himself supplies the dessert, a gooseberry fool. The dish is wittily chosen, an honest acknowledgment that he was often and widely regarded as foolish in his talk and behavior, but also a just characterization of his writings. A gooseberry fool is a teasing, paradoxical confection, simultaneously sweet and sharp.

Notes and References

Chapter One

1. Katharine C. Balderston, *The History and Sources of Percy's Memoir of Goldsmith* (Cambridge: Cambridge University Press, 1926), 13; *The Collected Letters of Oliver Goldsmith*, ed. Katharine C. Balderston (Cambridge: Cambridge University Press, 1928), 162 (hereafter cited as *Letters*); James Prior, *The Life of Oliver Goldsmith*, M.B., 2 vols. (London, 1837), 1:14.

2. *Letters*, 163. Catherine's biographical sketch occupies pp. 162–77.

3. *Letters*, 33, 30, 37.

4. Balderston, *Percy's Memoir*, 12–13.

5. See Patrick Murray, "The Riddle of Goldsmith's Ancestry," *Studies* 63 (1974):177–90.

6. *Letters*, 58. Goldsmith's heavy gambling is recorded by William Cooke, "Table Talk," *European Magazine* 24 (1793), 172; and by Joseph Cradock, *Literary and Miscellaneous Memoirs*, 4 vols. (London, 1828), 1:232.

7. *Letters*, 29–30; *Collected Works of Oliver Goldsmith*, 5 vols., ed. Arthur Friedman (Oxford: Clarendon Press, 1966), 1:385—hereafter cited in the text by volume and page number and referred to in subsequent notes as *Works*; *Portraits by Sir Joshua Reynolds*, ed. F. W. Hilles (London: Heinemann, 1952), 45.

8. Prior, *Life* 1:23.

9. *Works* 2:114.

10. Balderston, *Percy's Memoir*, 14.

11. Reported by Prior, *Life* 1:32.

12. The episode is narrated by Catherine, in *Letters*, 166–68. It is likely that this fine story was improved in the telling—by Goldsmith, or by Catherine, or by both.

13. *Letters*, 59.

14. Prior, *Life* 1:69.

15. *Letters*, xxix; the story is on pp. 170–76.

16. Stephen Gwynn, *Memorials of an Eighteenth-Century Painter* [the painter is James Northcote] (London, 1898), 96.

17. *Letters*, 176; Prior, *Life* 1:105, citing Catherine.

18. This paragraph draws on *Letters*, 28, 30, 58, 51, 53; "The Deserted Village," lines 41–48, 130–32, 194; *An History of the Earth and Animated Nature*, 8 vols. (London, 1774), 6:1–5, 32.

19. *Letters*, 6.

20. John Forster, *The Life and Times of Oliver Goldsmith*, 2 vols., 2d ed. (London, 1854), 1:54.

21. Thomas Percy, "The Life of Dr. Oliver Goldsmith," in *The Miscellaneous Works of Oliver Goldsmith, M.B.*, 4 vols. (London, 1801), 1:21.

22. *Letters*, 10–11.

23. *Letters*, 13.

24. *Letters*, 18, 17.

25. *Letters*, 24.

26. See *Sale Catalogues of Libraries of Eminent Persons*, ed. A. N. L. Munby, vol. 7, *Poets and Men of Letters*, ed. Hugh Amory (London: Mansell, 1973), 227–46.

27. *Works* 1:284. See Keith Brown, "A Kind of Comradeship: Goldsmith and the Late Famous Baron Holberg," *English Studies* 61 (1980): 37–46.

28. *Letters*, 32.

29. Ralph M. Wardle, *Oliver Goldsmith* (Lawrence: University of Kansas Press, 1957), 65.

30. *The History of the Robinhood Society* (London, 1764), 193.

31. *Letters*, 44.

32. John Evans, "Goldsmith and William: Two Original Anecdotes," *European Magazine* 53 (1808): 373.

33. Cooke, "Table Talk," 91–92.

34. *Works* 1:458. In *The Vicar of Wakefield* George Primrose's cousin tersely lists the tribulations of an usher's life; see *Works* 4:107–8.

35. John Ginger suggests that Goldsmith may have been deceived by the promises (for which he would have paid) of the kind of impostor who was later to figure in his works; see *The Notable Man: The Life and Times of Oliver Goldsmith* (London: Hamish Hamilton, 1977), 106–8.

36. The text of Johnson's Latin epitaph is given in James Boswell, *Life of Johnson*, edited by R. W. Chapman, revised by J. D. Fleeman (London: Oxford University Press, 1980), 778–79.

37. *Letters*, 52.

38. Boswell, *Life of Johnson*, 563.

39. Boswell, *Life of Johnson*, 411.

40. Prior, *Life* 2:359.

41. *Letters*, 3, 8, 40–41.

42. Boswell, *Life of Johnson*, 292; John Wooll, *Biographical Memoirs of Joseph Warton* (London, 1806), 312–13; Reynolds, *Portraits*, 43.

43. *Works* 3:354–55; Reynolds, *Portraits*, 46–48.

44. Reynolds, *Portraits*, 46,44.

45. Cooke, "Table Talk," 259.

46. *Works* 2:194; *Letters*, 50.

47. Boswell, *Life of Johnson*, 545.

48. James Northcote, *The Life of Sir Joshua Reynolds*, 2 vols., 2d. ed. (London, 1818), 1:248; Northcote is reporting Reynolds.

49. Reynolds, *Portraits*, 42–44.

Chapter Two

1. Horace, Epistle 2.1 ("To Augustus"), 210 ff. In his essay "A Dream" Goldsmith slyly pictures Horace gazing with admiration at the prowess of Pindar, "this literary rope-dancer"; see *Works* 3:126.

2. *Works* 2:413–14. Goldsmith had used this verse form, with its bathetic final line, in the elegy "On that glory of her sex, Mrs. Mary Blaize" (*Works* 1:433–34), and was to reemploy it in the first three stanzas of the "Elegy on the Death of a Mad Dog" (*Works* 4:88). He took the device from a mock-elegy in French, "Le fameux La Galisse."

3. Prior, *Life* 2:127–28.

4. Prior, *Life* 2:291; Boswell, *Life of Johnson*, 293.

5. Gwynn, *Memorials of an Eighteenth-Century Painter*, 90–91.

6. Cooke, "Table Talk," 261.

7. James Boswell, *Boswell's Journal of a Tour to the Hebrides with Samuel Johnson*, ed. Frederick A. Pottle and Charles H. Bennett (New York: Viking Press, 1936), 238.

8. *Letters*, 12.

9. *Letters*, 43–44.

10. Robert H. Hopkins, *The True Genius of Oliver Goldsmith* (Baltimore: Johns Hopkins University Press, 1969), 61–63.

11. Boswell, *Life of Johnson*, 778–79, 527.

12. Robert D. Mayo, *The English Novel in the Magazines, 1740–1815* (Evanston, Ill.: Northwestern University Press, 1962), 226. Mayo cites the *London Magazine* for 1779.

13. Hopkins, *True Genius*, 96.

Chapter Three

1. *Works* 2:19–20. All quotations from *The Citizen of the World* follow the text of the first (1762) edition.

2. *Letters*, 5.

3. Wardle, *Goldsmith*, 113.

4. Prior, *Life* 1:360.

5. Boswell, *Life of Johnson*, 1081.

6. Jonathan Swift, *Gulliver's Travels*, book 3, chap. 10.

7. *Works* 2:74. This sentence is taken verbatim from Johnson's "Observations on the Present State of Affairs" (*Literary Magazine*, 1756), an anonymous essay of whose authorship Goldsmith was probably unaware.

8. Leon Radzinowicz, *A History of English Criminal Law*, 4 vols. (London: Stevens, 1948–56), 1:4–5, 148. Approximately two-thirds of the death sentences were carried out.

9. Hopkins, *True Genius*, 119.

10. Margaret Anne Doody, *The Daring Muse: Augustan Poetry Reconsidered* (Cambridge: Cambridge University Press, 1985), especially chaps. 1 and 5.

11. *Works* 3:191. I quote throughout from the second (1766) edition of the *Essays*, Goldsmith's final version, revised and enlarged.

Chapter Four

1. *Letters*, 63.

2. Cooke, "Table Talk," 171.

3. Boswell, *Life of Johnson*, 918, 511. Reynolds similarly comments that "Goldsmith's mind was entirely unfurnished"; see *Portraits*, 50.

4. Samuel Johnson, *Lives of the English Poets*, 3 vols., ed. George Birkbeck Hill (Oxford: Clarendon Press, 1905), 2:49.

5. *Critical Review*, July 1770; cited in *Works* 3:402.

6. Horace, Ode 4, 12:27–28: "misce stultitiam consiliis brevem; / dulce est desipere in loco." In *Tom Jones* Fielding comments on Garrick's "sometimes condescending to play the fool" (as he would later do with Goldsmith), and cites the precedents of Scipio and Laelius (book 7, chap. 1). Goldsmith had reminded his brother Henry in 1759 that "It is a Good remark of Montaign's that the wisest men often have friends with whom they do not care how much they play the fool" (*Letters*, 65).

7. Reynolds, *Portraits*, 42.

8. Cooke, "Table Talk," 93.

9. *Works* 4:334.

10. Neither the account of Boyle nor that of Regnard can be confidently ascribed to Goldsmith, and Arthur Friedman excludes the latter (published in the *Weekly Magazine*, 5 January 1760) from the *Collected Works*. Since it has many of the hallmarks of Goldsmith's style, I am inclined to accept it as his.

11. *Letters*, 63.

12. "*The Idler*" and "*The Adventurer*," vol. 2 in *The Yale Edition of the Works of Samuel Johnson*, ed. W. J. Bate, John M. Bullitt, and L. F. Powell (New Haven: Yale University Press, 1963), 262.

13. Johnson, *Lives of the Poets* 2:332. Friedman notes the debt to Johnson in *Works* 5:45–46.

14. *Works* 3:379ff. Prior suspected that Goldsmith had written the letter. Roger Lonsdale's discovery, in the *Weekly Magazine* for 26 January 1760, of a letter about gamesters that anticipates the phrasing of "Nash's" letter, confirms the suspicion: see "Goldsmith and *The Weekly Magazine*: The Missing Numbers," *Review of English Studies*, n.s. 37 (1986): 223–24.

Chapter Five

1. *Works* 1:17, 57; see also 1:5, 21, 23.

2. The novel is described as "this very singular Tale" in the *Monthly Review*,

May 1766 (cited in *Works* 4:9). Schlegel and Carlyle saw it as romance and idyll; see G. S. Rousseau, ed., *Goldsmith: The Critical Heritage* (London: Routledge and Kegan Paul, 1974), 62, 280. For *The Vicar of Wakefield* as satire, see W. O. S. Sutherland, *The Art of the Satirist* (Austin: University of Texas Press, 1965), 84–91; Richard J. Jaarsma, "Satiric Intent in *The Vicar of Wakefield*," *Studies in Short Fiction* 5 (1968): 331–41; Hopkins, *True Genius*, chap. 5. Johnson's verdict is recorded by Fanny Burney; see *The Diary and Letters of Madame D'Arblay*, ed. Charlotte Barrett, with additional notes by Austin Dobson (London: Macmillan, 1904–5), 1:77. For Ricardo Quintana's judgment see his *Oliver Goldsmith, a Georgian Study* (New York: Macmillan, 1967), 115.

3. John Butt, *The Mid-Eighteenth Century*, edited and completed by Geoffrey Carnall (Oxford: Clarendon Press, 1979), 475.

4. This contrast is pointed out by Oliver W. Ferguson in "Dr. Primrose and Goldsmith's Clerical Ideal," *Philological Quarterly* 54 (1975): 327. Others are noted by MacDonald Emslie, *Goldsmith: "The Vicar of Wakefield"* (London: Edward Arnold, 1963), 56, and Sven Bäckman, *This Singular Tale: A Study of "The Vicar of Wakefield" and Its Literary Background* (Lund, Sweden: C. W. K. Gleerup, 1971), 40 ff.

5. D. W. Jefferson, "Observations on *The Vicar of Wakefield*," *Cambridge Journal* 3 (1949–50): 626. Jefferson is discussing the general effect of conventional elements in the eighteenth-century novel.

6. Sheldon Sacks, *Fiction and the Shape of Belief: A Study of Henry Fielding* (Berkeley and Los Angeles: University of California Press, 1964), 8.

7. A cruder version of the whipper whipped occurs in a late essay, "A Register of Scotch Marriages" (*Works* 3:219).

8. T. S. Eliot, "Poetry in the Eighteenth Century," in Boris Ford, ed., *The Pelican Guide to English Literature*, vol. 4, *From Dryden To Johnson* (Harmondsworth: Penguin, 1957), 275.

9. Hopkins, *True Genius*, 204–5.

10. Robert Hopkins is very severe on the Vicar for his use of the word "treasure"; see *True Genius*, 185–86, 210–12, 220. His argument is countered by Irvin Ehrenpreis, *Literary Meaning and Augustan Values* (Charlottesville: University of Virginia Press, 1974), 31–33, and by Thomas R. Preston, "The Uses of Adversity: Worldly Detachment and Heavenly Treasure in *The Vicar of Wakefield*," *Studies in Philology* 81 (1984): 232–36.

11. Frances Sheridan, *The Memoirs of Miss Sidney Bidulph* 3 vols. (London, 1761), 2:321–22; J. M. S. Tompkins, *The Popular Novel in England, 1770–1800* (London: Constable, 1932), 109.

12. Sarah Fielding, *The Adventures of David Simple*, ed. Malcolm Kelsall (London: Oxford University Press, 1969), 311; see also pp. 384, 414.

13. Sheridan, *Sidney Bidulph* 1:5; 2:102, 413.

14. William Black, *Oliver Goldsmith* (London, 1878), 87; Martin C.

Battestin, *The Providence of Wit: Aspects of Form in Augustan Literature and the Arts* (Oxford: Clarendon Press, 1974), 193–214.

15. Battestin, *Providence of Wit*, 208.

16. Eric Rothstein and Howard D. Weinbrot, "The Vicar of Wakefield, Mr. Wilmot, and the 'Whistonean Controversy,' " *Philological Quarterly* 55 (1976): 226–27.

17. Hopkins, *True Genius*, 191.

18. Wayne C. Booth, *The Rhetoric of Fiction* (Chicago: University of Chicago Press, 1961), 311 ff.

19. Emslie, *Vicar of Wakefield*, 24.

20. Hopkins, *True Genius*, 216.

21. Clive T. Probyn, *English Fiction of the Eighteenth Century, 1700–1789* (Harlow, Essex, England: Longman, 1987), 157.

22. Battestin, *Providence of Wit*, 196.

Chapter Six

1. Boswell, *Life of Johnson*, 513–14.

2. David Hume, *Essays and Treatises on Several Subjects. A New Edition*, 4 vols. (London, 1760), 2:25. The second volume of these essays was first published in 1752.

3. Hume, *Essays* 2:38.

4. R. S. Crane, "The 'Deserted Village' in Prose (1762)," *Times Literary Supplement*, 8 September 1927, p. 607.

5. John Sekora, *Luxury: The Concept in Western Thought, Eden to Smollett* (Baltimore: Johns Hopkins University Press, 1977), 102.

6. Pat Rogers, "The Dialectic of *The Traveller*," in *The Art of Oliver Goldsmith*, ed. Andrew Swarbrick (London: Vision, 1984), 118–21.

7. *Gentleman's Magazine*, December 1764, in Rousseau, *Critical Heritage*, 33.

8. "A Prospect of Society" was erroneously printed in reverse order; it was withdrawn from publication at the last moment, giving Goldsmith the opportunity for considerable revision. Its text can be reconstituted from the notes in *Works* 4:248–68, or read more conveniently in a Scolar Press reprint (Menston, Yorkshire, England, 1970).

9. Roger Lonsdale aptly cites Johnson's *Dictionary*, *s.v.* "long": "Longing; desirous; or perhaps long continued, from the disposition to continue looking at anything desired"; see *The Poems of Thomas Gray, William Collins, Oliver Goldsmith*, ed. Roger Lonsdale (London: Longman, 1969), 656.

10. Anne Williams, *Prophetic Strain: The Greater Lyric in the Eighteenth Century* (Chicago: Chicago University Press, 1984), 117.

11. John Montague, "The Sentimental Prophecy: A Study of *The Deserted Village*," in Swarbrick, *Art of Goldsmith*, 104.

12. Percy, "Life," in *Miscellaneous Works of Goldsmith* 1:113.

Chapter Seven

1. *Oliver Goldsmith: The Grumbler*, ed. Alice I. Perry Wood (Cambridge: Harvard University Press, 1931), xviii; the scene is on pp. 11–12.

2. Wardle, *Goldsmith*, 227.

3. Letter to Lady Ossory, 14 December 1773, in *The Yale Edition of Horace Walpole's Correspondence*, 48 vols., ed. W. S. Lewis et al., vol. 32 (New Haven: Yale University Press, 1965), 170–71.

4. Boswell, *Life of Johnson*, 384–85.

5. Fielding, *Tom Jones*, book 11, chap. 1; book 5, chap. 1.

6. Thomas Wilkes, *A General View of the Stage* (London, 1759), 39–41. John Hill says that critics give "a vast preference" to genteel comedy; see *The Actor* (London, 1755), 269–70.

7. Boswell, *Life of Johnson*, 389.

8. Samuel Johnson, *The Rambler*, vol. 3 of *The Yale Edition of the Works of Samuel Johnson*, ed. W. J. Bate and Albrecht B. Strauss (New Haven: Yale University Press, 1969), 314–15.

9. *Works* 3:213. Goldsmith may once again be echoing Fielding. In *The Author's Farce* (revised version, 1750) Marplay (Theophilus Cibber) brags of having written a humorless comedy containing a "scene of tender, melancholy conversation"; see Henry Fielding, *The Author's Farce*, ed. Charles B. Woods (Lincoln: University of Nebraska Press, 1966), 85.

10. Goldsmith draws on the alehouse discussion that follows an applauded puppet-show performance of a version of *The Provoked Husband* from which all the vulgar (that is, comic) material has been omitted; see Henry Fielding, *Tom Jones*, book 13, chap. 5.

Epilogue

1. *Letters*, 127.

2. *An History of the Earth*, 4:2.

3. *An History of the Earth*, 8:65–95 (bees); 6:320 (dragonflies); 6:32 (lapwing); 6:1–5 (bittern); 5:231–34 (rooks); 5:207 (partridge); 3:8–9 (cow).

4. The phrase is Rachel Trickett's, referring to the departure from Auburn; see " 'Curious Eye': Some Aspects of Visual Description in Eighteenth-Century Literature," in *Augustan Studies: Essays in Honor of Irvin Ehrenpreis*, ed. Douglas L. Patey and T. Keegan (Newark: University of Delaware Press, 1985), 245.

5. *The Grecian History*, 2 vols. (London, 1774), 1:19–20, 147–48.

6. *Letters*, 34.

7. Hopkins, *True Genius*, 11.

Selected Bibliography

PRIMARY WORKS

Collected Works of Oliver Goldsmith. Edited by Arthur Friedman. 5 vols. Oxford: Clarendon Press, 1966. The authoritative, old-spelling edition. Does not include historical writings, adaptations, and translations.

Oliver Goldsmith: The Grumbler. Edited by Alice I. Perry Wood. Cambridge: Harvard University Press, 1931.

The Poems of Thomas Gray, William Collins, Oliver Goldsmith. Edited by Roger Lonsdale. London: Longman, 1969. The poems of Goldsmith, superbly annotated, occupy pp. 567–769.

The Collected Letters of Oliver Goldsmith. Edited by Katharine C. Balderston. Cambridge: Cambridge University Press, 1928.

SECONDARY WORKS

Bibliographies

F[riedman], A[rthur], "Oliver Goldsmith." In *The New Cambridge Bibliography of English Literature,* 5 vols., edited by George Watson, 2:1191–210. Cambridge: Cambridge University Press, 1971. A comprehensive list of Goldsmith's writings and editions of his works, and of biographical and critical material published between 1761 and 1969.

Woods, Samuel H. *Oliver Goldsmith: A Reference Guide.* Boston: G. K. Hall, 1982. A fully annotated, though not fully comprehensive, list of writings about Goldsmith and his works, from 1759 to 1978.

Books and Articles

Bäckman, Sven. *This Singular Tale: A Study of "The Vicar of Wakefield" and Its Literary Background.* Lund Studies in English, no. 40. Lund, Sweden: G. W. K. Gleerup, 1971. Relates the novel to the traditions of prose fiction, the periodical essay, and the drama; analyzes structure and draws interesting parallels with Goldsmith's other writings.

Battestin, Martin C. "Goldsmith: The Comedy of Job." In *The Providence of Wit: Aspects of Form in Augustan Literature and the Arts,* 193–214. Oxford:

Clarendon Press, 1974. A cogent demonstration of the analogies between *The Vicar of Wakefield* and the Book of Job.

Bevis, Richard. *The Laughing Tradition: Stage Comedy in Garrick's Day.* Athens: University of Georgia Press, 1980. A valuable reassessment of "sentimental" and "laughing" comedy (chaps. 3 and 5), and an appreciative view of *She Stoops to Conquer* (pp. 205–14).

Bloom, Harold, ed. *Oliver Goldsmith.* Modern Critical Views Series. New York: Chelsea House, 1987. A stimulating collection: 11 pieces, concentrating on Goldsmith's major works, originally published between 1967 and 1984—but here shorn of their footnotes.

Booth, Wayne C. " 'The Self-Portraiture of Genius': *The Citizen of the World* and Critical Method." *Modern Philology* 73 (1976), Supplement to honor Arthur Friedman, S85–96. Also in Harold Bloom, *Oliver Goldsmith*, 21–35. Skillful defense of Goldsmith's "art of the miscellaneous"; stresses the importance for the reader of the authorial presence.

Dussinger, John A. *The Discourse of the Mind in Eighteenth-Century Fiction.* The Hague: Mouton, 1974. The intellectual background to Goldsmith's identity problem (chap. 1), and a trenchant reading of *The Vicar of Wakefield* (chap. 5).

————."Philanthropy and the Selfish Reader in Goldsmith's *Life of Nash.*" *Studies in Burke and His Time* 19 (1978): 197–207. A judiciously balanced account. Goldsmith's wit is directed against both Nash and those readers who are lacking in humanity.

Emslie, MacDonald. *Goldsmith: "The Vicar of Wakefield."* Studies in English Literature no. 9. London: Edward Arnold, 1963. Emphasizes Goldsmith's problems with his narrative mode, and the reader's consequent "difficulties of assessment."

Ferguson, Oliver W. "Antisentimentalism in Goldsmith's *The Good-Natured Man*: The Limits of Parody." In *The Dress of Words: Essays on Restoration and Eighteenth-Century Literature in Honor of Richmond P. Bond*, edited by Robert B. White, 105–16. Lawrence: University of Kansas Press, 1978. Also in Harold Bloom, *Oliver Goldsmith*, 37–48. Argues that Goldsmith is not attacking or parodying genteel, sentimental comedy in *The Good-Natured Man*, but simply rejecting it.

————."Oliver Goldsmith: The Personality of the Essayist." *Philological Quarterly* 61 (1982): 179–92. A detailed study of how Goldsmith exploited his essentially attractive personality.

Gallaway, W. F. "The Sentimentalism of Goldsmith." *PMLA* 48 (1933): 1167–81. A careful estimate.

Golden, Morris. "The Broken Dream of *The Deserted Village.*" *Literature and Psychology* 9 (1959): 41–44. The innocence of Auburn, a specifically female innocence, is that of a now irrecoverable childhood.

Ginger, John. *The Notable Man: The Life and Times of Oliver Goldsmith.* London: Hamish Hamilton, 1977. An expansive and sensitive (though not always scholarly) biography.

Heilman, Robert B. "The Sentimentalism of Goldsmith's *Good-Natured Man*." In *Studies for William A. Read*, edited by Nathaniel M. Caffee and Thomas A. Kirby, 237–53. Baton Rouge: Louisiana State University Press, 1940. Cogently defends the play against the charge of sentimentality; Goldsmith ridicules the typical sentimental hero and shows the importance of moral discrimination.

Hilles, F. W., ed. *Portraits by Sir Joshua Reynolds*. Yale Editions of the Private Papers of James Boswell, 27–59. New York: McGraw-Hill; London: Heinemann, 1952. Brief but penetrating account by the contemporary who knew Goldsmith best.

Hopkins, Robert H. *The True Genius of Oliver Goldsmith*. Baltimore: Johns Hopkins University Press, 1969. Emphasizes the "tough-minded," satirical Goldsmith, the champion of good sense against sentiment.

Hume, Robert D. "Goldsmith and Sheridan and the Supposed Revolution of 'Laughing' against 'Sentimental' Comedy." In *The Rakish Stage: Studies in English Drama, 1660–1800*, 312–55. Carbondale: Southern Illinois University Press, 1983. A clear-sighted corrective to Goldsmith's own partial view of the development of comic drama during his lifetime. First published in 1972.

Lonsdale, Roger. " 'A Garden and a Grave': The Poetry of Oliver Goldsmith." In *The Author in His Work: Essays on a Problem in Criticism*, edited by Louis L. Martz and Aubrey Williams, 3–30. New Haven: Yale University Press, 1978. Also in Harold Bloom, *Oliver Goldsmith*, 49–72. A subtle and persuasive consideration of the "personal voice" in "The Traveller" and "The Deserted Village."

Mullan, John. *Sentiment and Sociability: The Language of Feeling in the Eighteenth Century*, 136–46. Oxford: Clarendon Press, 1988. Sees Goldsmith, in *The Vicar of Wakefield*, largely accepting the conventions of the novel of sensibility.

Probyn, Clive T. *English Fiction of the Eighteenth Century, 1700–1789*, 152–60. Harlow, Essex, England: Longman, 1987. A concise, acute analysis of *The Vicar of Wakefield*.

Quintana, Ricardo. *Oliver Goldsmith, a Georgian Study*. New York: Macmillan, 1967. Considers every aspect of Goldsmith's work with graceful enthusiasm.

Rousseau, G. S., ed. *Goldsmith: The Critical Heritage*. London: Routledge and Kegan Paul, 1974. The critical response to Goldsmith from the earliest reviews to 1912; helpfully generous extracts, especially from eighteenth- and early nineteenth-century critics and commentators.

Swarbrick, Andrew, ed. *The Art of Oliver Goldsmith*. London: Vision Press, 1984. A collection of essays on almost all aspects of Goldsmith's work, including the *History of the Earth* (seen as an example of the picturesque mode). Particularly valuable on *The Citizen of the World* and the poems.

Wardle, Ralph M. *Oliver Goldsmith*. Lawrence: University of Kansas Press, 1957. Sympathetic and reliable biography.

Index

The Author

Peter Dixon is professor of English at Queen Mary and Westfield College, University of London. He was an undergraduate at Oxford and did post-graduate work at Royal Holloway College, London. After holding lecturing posts at the University of Adelaide and Queen's University, Belfast, he joined the English Department at Queen Mary College, later moving as reader to Westfield College.

He is the author of *The World of Pope's Satires* and an introduction to rhetoric in the Routledge Critical Idiom Series. He has prepared editions of Goldsmith's poetry, Swift's *Gulliver's Travels* (with John Chalker), Cibber and Vanbrugh's *The Provoked Husband*, and Farquhar's *Recruiting Officer*.